Halsgrove • Dartmoor National Park Authority

DARTMOOR ARTISTS

Brian Le Messurier

Halsgrove • Dartmoor National Park Authority

DARTMOOR ARTISTS

Brian Le Messurier

First published in Great Britain in 2002

British Library Cataloguing-in-Publication Data
A CIP record for this title is available from the British Library

ISBN 1 84114 165 8

HALSGROVE

Halsgrove House
Lower Moor Way
Tiverton, Devon EX16 6SS
Tel: 01884 243242
Fax: 01884 243325
email sales@halsgrove.com
website www.halsgrove.com

Printed and bound in Italy by Centro Grafico Ambrosiano, Milan

Foreword

The British countryside has formed the backdrop to some of our finest novels and has inspired some of our greatest prose, poetry, music, sculpture, and long tradition of landscape art.

Dartmoor has attracted the aesthetic attention of some of the more famous art masters, such as J M W Turner, and has nurtured its own Devon-born greats. There has also been a plethora of other artists inspired by this special place and together these have unwittingly, quietly, built up a body of art justly worthy of greater public attention and appreciation. Through their work we see that landscapes are far more than places; they are events and experiences and we see not only romantic views of seemingly natural environments and elements but also the reality of eking livelihoods from both on and under the surface.

Art can influence the way we think about our natural and cultural environments. Fifty years have passed since the creation of Dartmoor as a National Park. It is worth reflecting that nineteenth-century painters who ventured into the wildernesses of the United States made significant contributions to the origin and development of the world-wide national parks movement. In particular, I am reminded of the art of Thomas Moran, including a series of beautiful watercolours, that strongly influenced public opinion towards the establishment of Yellowstone in 1872 as the world's first National Park.

Dartmoor's atmosphere, its horizons, swollen rivers, granitic forms, cloud shadows and broken light, the nature of place and the place of nature, cultural interfaces and processes, and our personal responses – all can provide the creative stimulus. It is heartening to see a continuing tradition of Dartmoor landscape art. We now see a new genre of inspired and talented artists whose close observations, whose skills and respect and reverence for nature, and the ability to interpret our impact upon it, are helping to portray the character of the region. Their art itself can become a part of our diverse heritage.

Nick Atkinson
National Park Officer
Dartmoor National Park Authority

Contents

Acknowledgements

I am grateful to numerous people for help in many ways in the preparation of this book, but my major indebtedness is to John Biggs of the art dealers J Collins & Son of Bideford, who allowed me to borrow pictures from his photographic archive for illustrative purposes. I thank him most warmly.

The undermentioned individuals were splendidly co-operative. I thank them all: David Anthony, June Ashburner, Jane Baker, Robin Barlow, Hugh Bedford, Chris Beetles, Stephen Braund, Roger Brien, Jamie Broughton, Simon Butler, Doreen Cardwell, Chris Chapman, Brian and Mary Chugg, Judith Cosford, Deborah Coxon, Susan Derges, Robin Fenner, Sue Freeman (Godolphin Fine Art), Anthony Greenstreet, Peter and Pauline Hamilton-Leggett, Simon Hill and family, Michael Honnor, Ken Howard RA, Dr Peter Howard, Penelope Lively, Michael Morgan RI, Professor Brendan Neiland RA, Ken Nott, Michael and Gil O' Reilly, Graham Ovenden, G H Robertson Owen, Jenny Pery, John Radford, Bill Ransom, Ken and Jenny Sanders, Nick Skeaping, Dr Sam Smiles, the late John Somers Cocks, Chris Trant (Mill Gallery), Christine Trigger, Pete Webb and John Weir.

Likewise I thank the following organisations for their assistance: the Devon & Exeter Institution, the Devonshire Association (Dr Tom Greeves), the Catherine Linehan Memorial Fund, Mount House School, Plymouth Museum & Art Gallery (Maureen Attrill), Royal Albert Memorial Museum & Art Gallery, Tavistock Golf Club, University of Plymouth Art College Library, and Dartmoor National Park Authority.

Brian Le Messurier

December 2002

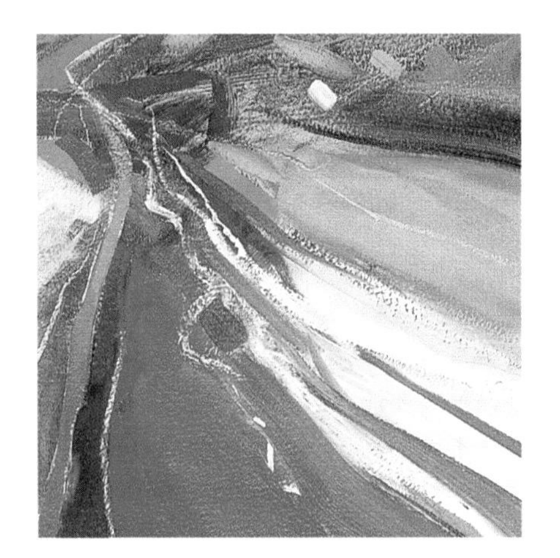

Introduction

In his editorial introduction to *Dartmoor: A New Study* in 1970 Crispin Gill remarked on certain aspects of Dartmoor's history which had not been dealt with by the contributors he had assembled. After dealing with Dartmoor books and commenting on the novelists in a few lines, he wrote dismissively of the artists thus:

> *Nor have the painters been dealt with, but as with too many of the novels, one has the feeling that they have only a superficial understanding of the moor, and add little to one's knowledge or appreciation.*

Thirty years later it is possible to correct this omission by the publication of the present book. In the intervening period a considerable amount of research and authorial endeavour has put much information about Dartmoor artists in print, making for a better-informed reading public. Five books in particular have helped in this widening of understanding and should be mentioned at the start of this survey.

Several years of painstaking research by John Somers Cocks produced *Devon Topographical Prints 1660–1870, A Catalogue and Guide,* in 1977, an invaluable resource for anyone wanting to know what prints are available on a parish by parish basis, and the identity of the artists and the engravers or lithographers.

Jane Baker, in 1988 the Curator of Fine Art at the Royal Albert Memorial Museum & Art Gallery in Exeter, wrote a handsomely-produced book called *A Vision of Dartmoor: Paintings of F J Widgery 1861–1942*, and combined with it a survey of other significant Dartmoor artists.

The third is Peter Howard's *Landscapes: The Artists' Vision* which was published in 1991. This book uses material collected by the author in the course of his PhD thesis research, and although it has a country-wide application, it possesses an undeniable West Country, even Devon, bias. He analyses how artists looked at the landscape, and how different kinds of countryside became more fashionable to paint with the passing of time.

The collector will want to have access to *Hidden Talents: A Dictionary of Neglected Artists Working 1880–1950,* compiled and published by Jeremy Wood in 1994, which is just what it says. Over 1500 lesser known artists are listed, with helpful pocket biographies and ten illustrations of Dartmoor subjects.

Lastly, the catalogue of the ground-breaking exhibition *The Perfection of England: Artist Visitors to Devon c.1750–1870,* which was put together by Sam Smiles and Michael Pidgley and exhibited at the Royal Albert Memorial Museum in 1995, is a most useful account of the nationally-known painters who came to Devon, and were inspired by what they saw to leave us examples of their work. Nearly every painting shown at the exhibition is illustrated in the catalogue, together with a scholarly commentary.

There have been other publications in recent years, but these are the chief general titles. Perhaps the surprising thing is that there has been nothing substantial published about Devon artists since George Pycroft's *Art in Devonshire* appeared as long ago as 1883. (Though we should mention W G Hoskins' 6½ page piece in his *Devon* of 1954.) Initially *Art in Devonshire* was printed in two parts in the *Transactions* of the Devonshire Association for the Advancement of Science, Literature and Art for 1881 and 1882, and published again in 1883 as a separate revised book. Perhaps an 'Association for the Advancement of Science, Literature and Art' should put more emphasis on the last of its stated aims. However, at its 2000 Annual General Meeting and Millennium Conference the Association included a paper by Jenny Pery, 'The Visionary

Gleam: Contemporary Artists and the Devon Landscape', which greatly illuminated our view of the art scene at the present time.

This book sprang from a paper originally commissioned by the Dartmoor National Park Authority in 1991 to pass to the exhibition designers preparing the displays for the High Moorland Visitor Centre at Princetown. The original essay is now vastly expanded, updated and illustrated. The National Park Authority commissioned this expanded research and the writing of the text for this publication. The Visitor Centre is itself playing a part in the cultural life of the National Park by providing exhibition display space for pictures and photographs, sculptures and crafts.

The Dartmoor artistic scene is thriving, and the difficulty for the contemporary commentator is in selection.

Abbreviations found in this book

ACC Antique Collectors' Club
AFAS Armed Forces Art Society
AOWS Associate of the 'Old' Society of Painters in Watercolour
ARA Associate of the Royal Academy
ARCA Associate of the Royal College of Art
ARSA Associate of the Royal Scottish Academy
ARWS Associate of the Royal Society of Painters in Watercolours
BWS British Watercolour Society
CBE Commander of the British Empire
DL Deputy Lieutenant
fl Flourished, exhibited
FGS Fellow of the Geological Society
FRCS Fellow of the Royal College of Surgeons
FRHS Fellow of the Royal Horticultural Society
FRIBA Fellow, Royal Institute of British Architects
FRSE Fellow, Royal Society of Edinburgh
FSA Fellow of the Society of Antiquities
GNRP Great Norden Railway Publications
JP Justice of the Peace
JVSC John V Somers Cocks *Devon Topograpical Prints*
KCMG Knight Commander, Order of St Michael and St George
KCVO Knight Commander, Royal Victorian Order
MA Master of Arts
Mallalieu *The Dictionary of British Watercolour Artists up to 1920* (see Bibliography)
NEAC New English Art Club
NWS New Society of Painters in Watercolours (founded 1831, RI from 1881)
OBE Order of the British Empire
OM Order of Merit
OWS 'Old' Society of Painters in Watercolours
POWS President of the 'Old' Society of Painters in Watercolours
PRA President of the Royal Academy
Pycroft *Art in Devonshire* (see Bibliography)
RA Royal Academician
RAMM Royal Albert Memorial Musem (and Art Gallery), Exeter
RBA Royal Society of British Artists
RBC Royal British Colonial Society of Artists
RCA Royal College of Art
RE Royal Society of Painter Etchers
RHA Royal Hibernian Academy
RI Royal Institute of Painters in Watercolours
SEA Society of Equestrian Artists
V & A Victoria & Albert Museum

Note: Although this book has a conventional index, to facilitate reference, the first and main entry of an artist is printed in a bold typeface. They appear in the book in approximate chronological order of Dartmoor association.

Well-known artists visit Dartmoor's fringes

The first attention given to Dartmoor by artists followed the writers and travellers who were themselves passing along the new roads and tracks opened up by the exploitation of the moor at the end of the eighteenth century.

The Grand Tour which so many young men had undertaken on the Continent during the century had given them a taste for travel and stimulated their artistic senses. Another driving force for those with artistic talent was the founding of the Royal Academy of Arts in 1768, and every year from 1769 its Summer Exhibition has been held. Until this time the artistic establishment rated landscape painting low in the hierarchy of genres, but the foundation of the Royal Academy gave it respectability.

It has to be stated at some stage, and the beginning of this book may be as good a place as any, that since people began painting Dartmoor there has been no 'Dartmoor School'. No *coterie* of like-minded artists has gathered together to portray the moorland scene in the way the Newlyn or Norwich Schools operated in their respective districts. But, as Professor W G Hoskins wrote in his *Devon* (Collins 1954, and subsequently reprinted), leaving Middlesex aside, 'Devon has produced more notable painters than any other county in England.' This does of course include portrait painters, miniaturists, and artists who never ventured on to Dartmoor, and are therefore beyond the terms of reference in this book.

Not surprisingly, Exeter and Plymouth were the two centres where artists, whether local or visiting, were based, and naturally enough, when two or three were active at the same time they made friends and probably shared transport arrangements. These relationships will be noted as and when they arise.

Dartmoor never attracted artists to the same extent as North Wales, the Lake District or the Scottish Highlands. The appreciation of high moorland scenery came late, between 1870 and 1910, in what may be called the Heroic period, and owed a good deal, so far as the West Country is concerned, to the popular appeal of *Lorna Doone*, R D Blackmore's romantic adventure story set on Exmoor and published in 1869.

The reader may be surprised to find how many notable English landscape artists painted on Dartmoor in the early years, though they tended to concentrate on the border villages and towns. Painters like Richard Wilson, Paul Sandby, Thomas Girtin, Thomas Rowlandson and J M W Turner had all painted on the moor by the early years of the nineteenth century. Truly, it was the national figures who led the way for the native talent to follow.

John Somers Cocks's catalogue *Devon Topographical Prints* lists 3502 prints under parishes for the county. After an 18-page introduction which explains the historical background, a couple of paragraphs may be taken to set the scene:

> *...it was not until the latter part of the eighteenth century that the natural British landscape came to be regarded at all. Without an appreciation of nature and the picturesque, the topographical print could at best only consist of views of important architecture, towns or antiquarian remains, with occasional scenes of military or naval importance.*
>
> *Once this landscape appreciation had begun it spread very rapidly, manifesting itself in contemporary prose and poetry as well as in art. There were a number of reasons for the phenomenon which cannot concern us here, but, at one stage at any rate, an impetus was given to it by the fact that during the wars with France travel on the Continent became impossible so that Englishmen who wished to tour or to winter in a mild climate were forced to do so in this country. Rather to their surprise perhaps, they found a great deal that they had previously overlooked, and Devon with its climate and fine and varied scenery soon came under their notice. Naturally they often required some memento of what they had seen, and the printsellers and artists were quick to fill their need. Individual prints, book illustrations and sets served to advertise the area still more, so that it becomes difficult to separate cause and effect by the early nineteenth century. But one has only to note the number of works that include the word picturesque in their titles to see what excited the admiration of the travellers in those years of discovery.*

This guide enables the present-day researcher to track down old views of the county, though it does not say where they may be found. The West Country Studies Library, Exeter, is a good starting point, followed by the Local History Section at Plymouth Central Library.

Lithograph 12 x 19cms entitled 'Bowerman's Nose from the E[ast]', by and after W. Spreat, c.1845.

A perusal of *Devon Topographical Prints* shows few examples of Dartmoor subjects before the end of the eighteenth century. The favoured moorland sites in the early years were fringe places like Okehampton Castle and the bridge at Ivybridge, both, probably, as they were easily seen from the coach routes to the west.

As this book was being written, Todd Gray published *Dartmoor Engraved* (The Mint Press 2001). This reproduces 246 images, though not all would qualify as 'art'. The section at the end of the book headed 'Military Manoeuvres in 1853 and 1873' includes pictures taken from *The Illustrated London News* and *The Graphic* which represent pre-photographic journalism. But two views of Ivybridge and 11 of Okehampton Castle bespeak their popularity, along with that of Lydford Gorge, as favourite border topics for artists.

It would appear that **John Inigo Richards RA (1731–1810)** is the earliest well-known artist to paint near Dartmoor. He painted an oil of Ivybridge in 1768 which is in the Tate Gallery, London, and he exhibited one of Okehampton Castle at the Royal Academy in 1770. He was a founder member of the Royal Academy, and its secretary from 1788 until his death.

Okehampton Castle was of course a picturesque ruin during the time when the picturesque was so much in vogue. Nature, and indeed man's works, were supposed to imitate art. It was also painted by artists with Classical leanings. These labels and dates cannot be too closely assigned as there was a good deal of overlap. No other Dartmoor subject has been painted by so many famous artists: Richard Wilson, J M W Turner, Francis Towne and Samuel Prout, and others, but this is jumping ahead. It helped that it was a rural castle; urban castles were less popular. It stands on a mound embowered in trees and ivy, and has a river running past. For J Walmesley in 1810 it lacked dramatic effect even so. He therefore added a lake at its foot, complete with sailing craft and fishermen.

Richard Wilson RA (1713?–1782) started life as a portraitist, but after spending several years in Italy he turned his hand to landscape paintings. Michael Pidgley suggests that his two square-format paintings of Lydford Waterfall and Okehampton Castle, now in different galleries in Cardiff and Manchester, were commissioned by Lord Courtenay in the early 1770s for a specific setting in Powderham Castle. The Courtenays did, of course, have connections with Okehampton Castle going back to Norman times. Sadly, the two Powderham Castle pictures were sold off, with others, in 1816. A different painting of Okehampton Castle by Wilson is now in Birmingham.

A copper engraving exists which suggests that **Paul Sandby RA (1725–1809)**, sometimes called 'the founder of British watercolour painting' came to Devon in 1780. It too shows Ivybridge, with the River Erme, a few buildings, and the moor rearing up to the north. A story is told in the pages of *The Western Antiquary* for December 1882 which probably relates to Okehampton Castle. The tale relates that a newly married couple journeyed to Okehampton from London on their honeymoon. They lodged in the town, and the husband being an artist set off upriver one day to 'exercise his pencil on the beauties of the scenery', as the account states.

He never came back, and despite a search by local people, no trace of him was ever found. The grieving widow returned to London, and in due course bore a son. Twenty years later the young man decided to see for himself where his father was lost. The account continues:

> *The son, in one of his rambles on the moor by the side of the West Okement, saw something glittering in the bed of the stream which excited his curiosity, and he essayed to get it out, and after some considerable trouble was successful in doing so, when it was discovered to be his father's box, which contained his papers. The story says that they were, from the water-tight fittings of the box, sufficiently preserved to identify the writings, and, painful to relate, not far from where the box was found were the bones of his lost father, more or less embedded in the bed of the stream.*

Yet another artist to paint Okehampton Castle was **Thomas Girtin (1775–1802)**, and a well-preserved small watercolour of 'Lydford Castle, Devon', signed and dated 1800, was sold at Sotheby's, London, for £176 000 in 1990. It has retained its original freshness because, as Susan Morris writes in *Sotheby's Art at Auction 1989–1990* (Sotheby's Publications 1990), it was found with another watercolour by Girtin of 'Jedburgh Abbey', presumably forgotten, at the bottom of a linen chest in the house of a descendant of Sir John Ramsden (1755–1839) who probably commissioned them. The picture is reproduced in the book mentioned above and also in *Antique Collecting* April 2001. As well as Lydford Castle, the church tower of Lydford parish church is shown, and in the background storm clouds pile up over the moor, while the sun illuminates the fields in the middle distance.

J M W Turner is supposed to have remarked of Girtin, 'If Tom had lived, I would have starved', for he died aged 27. However, about 800 works by Girtin are known, many of them faded in the sunlight of Victorian drawings rooms, which makes the Lydford and Jedburgh pictures so rare.

It was thought until 1996 that **Francis Towne (1740–1816)** had probably been born in Exeter, but documents have been discovered which locate his birthplace as Isleworth in Middlesex. For several years he was apprenticed and trained in various craft and painting skills, and in about 1763 he came to Exeter where he worked in the workshop of a coach painter.

He then made a shrewd career move, and set himself up as a drawing master, being particularly involved with the Merivale family. Exeter was a prosperous centre for professional people, and there were painting opportunities nearby. He had a chance to exhibit at the first Royal Academy exhibition in 1769 but declined, a decision he always regretted, as he failed on ten subsequent occasions to secure election.

FRANCIS TOWNE. 'Okehampton Castle' 1794. Pen, ink, pencil and watercolour 24 x 34cms.

COURTESY OF RAMM

Towne painted Okehampton Castle in 1772 and Canonteign Falls (in what we now know as the Dartmoor National Park) in 1773. He painted many pictures of Ugbrooke, Berry Pomeroy, Haldon House, Powderham Castle, Peamore and Great Fulford. In 1780 he toured and painted in Italy, moving to the Alps in 1781. The next tour was around the Lake District in 1786 with his friends James White and John Merivale, and numerous watercolours and sketchbooks survive from this tour.

On his return he alternated between London and Exeter, and in 1805 arranged a London exhibition devoted entirely to his pictures, about 200 in all. The cost of glass and frames meant that most pictures were simply pinned to the gallery walls. Timothy Wilcox the author of *Francis Towne* (Tate Gallery Publishing, 1997) who curated the 1997 exhibition at the Tate Gallery writes that 'Towne's singular venture appears to have passed unnoticed by artists and critics alike'.

Two years later he married a French dancer forty years his junior on what was probably his 68th birthday. Alas, they only had a few months of marriage as she died young and was buried at Heavitree in Exeter. Towne was 76 when he died. His last years were active, though he had a final painful illness. His body was brought back to Exeter to be with his wife, and although Heavitree parish church has been rebuilt, the gravestone, much worn, can be seen in the south aisle.

Francis Towne's paintings were forgotten at his death. Pycroft omits him from *Art in Devonshire* (1883), though an annotated copy in the Devon & Exeter Institution includes a short handwritten appendix. Between his death and 1818 three volumes of his mounted pictures were donated to the British Museum by his executor and friend, James White, and there they stayed, unregarded, until the publication of a British Museum catalogue in 1907.

A young man called Paul Oppé saw this, viewed the pictures, and shortly after spotted an uncatalogued bundle of watercolours in a saleroom, which including 17 signed by Towne. Oppé bought the lot for £1.25.

He was now led to the Merivale family who were still living at Barton Place on the outskirts of Exeter, and here he found nearly 300 of Towne's drawings. From his researches he wrote the first article about this elusive artist. (See Bibliography)

Towne's paintings are now greatly sought after. His style employed a limited range of colours, secure within a delicate pen outline which appeals to present-day connoisseurs. At a Phillips sale in January 1999 a small Towne watercolour of an Italian subject in greys, blues and greens was given an estimate of £8000 to £10 000. The actual selling price was £93 900.

The most prolific of late eighteenth century artists and a pioneer local painter was the **Reverend John Swete (1752–1821)**. He is well known as a diarist, for 17 of his illustrated journals have been published by Devon Books in four annual volumes since 1997.

Swete was born John Tripe in Ashburton, but inherited a fortune on condition he changed his name to Swete. He took Holy Orders in 1781, was briefly curate at Highweek and Kenn, and a prebendary at Exeter. In 1784 he married Charlotte Beaumont who he had met in Derbyshire while travelling to Scotland, and she bore him 14 children. They lived at Oxton House, near Kenn.

From 1789 to 1800 Swete travelled around Devon, and crossed the county boundary into Cornwall, Dorset and Somerset, criss-crossing Devon in every direction, and writing up his experiences in 20 volumes of journals. He illustrated the pages with neatly painted, somewhat naïve watercolours. Three of the volumes were lost in the Second World War and one of these was specifically about Dartmoor. He sometimes travelled with a friend, just occasionally with a member of his family, and probably always with a servant. He made notes and sketches at the time, and composed the finished article when he got home, often as a winter task. There are over 600 watercolours reproduced in full colour. They are not always

REVEREND JOHN SWETE 'East view of Fingle Bridge' 1797. Watercolour 19 x 25cms (below left). *'Tin Mines on Dartmoor' 1797. Watercolour.*
COURTESY DEVON COUNTY COUNCIL

REVEREND JOHN SWETE 'Beardown Farm' 1797. Watercolour 19 x 25cms.
COURTESY DEVON COUNTY COUNCIL

topographically accurate, and Swete was not above making a view or building more picturesque, though he was usually trying to paint in the Classical tradition. He had received some artistic tuition from William Payne (see *post*) and this is described in Todd Gray's perceptive introduction to the four volumes as recently published.

In common with his contemporaries Swete found moorland scenery:

> *...of the most dreary nature. The horizontal line on every quarter was formed by the hills and Torrs of Dartmoor – a wide waste where the eye found not a point to rest on – there was nothing picturesque, nor, though wild and rugged, was there anything romantic.*

Swete also painted scenes from his travels which he gave to friends, and these sometimes appear at auction.

Another artist, a professional topographical painter, but better known as a diarist, **Joseph Farington RA (1747–1821)**, called on Swete to get advice on places to visit in Devon, but as he heartily disliked moorland scenery, and considered the lower reaches of the rivers to be the scenes to paint – particularly the Dart and the Teign – he did not venture on to the high moor. However, it is suggested he may have painted at Buckland-in-the-Moor, Ashburton and Bovey Tracey in 1810. His diaries, published in 16 volumes by the Yale University Press, are interesting for the gossip and opinions expressed about other artists. He had a wide circle of acquaintances and was closely involved with the Royal Academy.

Sir William Elford (1748–1837), an amateur artist, and a senior partner in the banking firm of Elford, Tingcombe & Clark, lived on the western edge of Dartmoor, but did not paint much actually on the moor, although pictures of his of south-west Dartmoor are known. Elford was another Devon-based artist on whom Joseph Farington chose to call.

William Payne (1760–1830), as we have seen, knew Swete well, and they may have travelled together; they were of a similar age. Payne was born and died in London, but was based for some years in Plymouth where he worked as a draughtsman for the Board of Ordnance. While there he made several forays along the coast, up the River Tamar, and around the western fringe of Dartmoor to make the inevitable picture of Okehampton Castle. His painting of Brent Tor makes it appear like Mont Saint Michel in France, with a cart being led across a plain in the foreground resembling tidal flats. When he returned to London he became a drawing master, exhibited many pictures in oils and watercolours and travelled to Wales, the River Wye, and the Lake District. He is remembered as the inventor of Payne's grey.

WILLIAM PAYNE 'Oakhampton (sic) Castle & Town from the Park' c.1800. Watercolour 23.7 x 35cms (below left). *'Brent Torr' c.1800. Watercolour* (below). *'Harrow Bridge' c.1800* (bottom), *the place we now know as Horrabridge.*

COURTESY DEVON COUNTY COUNCIL

'Portrait of John White Abbott' c.1818–25. Oil on panel 16 x 13.9cms, by James Leakey (1775–1865). See page 37.

COURTESY OF RAMM

John White Abbott (1763–1851) was a pupil of Francis Towne. His uncle, James White, was Towne's solicitor, executor and friend, and Abbott's style closely followed that of the older man. He was born in Exeter, and became an apothecary and surgeon, so chose to be a dilettante painter who seems never to have sold one of his works, though he exhibited regularly at the Royal Academy. There is in the Victoria & Albert Museum a striking work of his called 'View near Canonteign – Devon', a scene also painted by Towne. Abbott regarded his work but lightly, and this particular painting was produced on a sheet made up of small pieces of paper stuck together in grid form, a device he sometimes resorted to if large sheets of paper were unavailable.

He travelled to Scotland and the Lake District, but appears not to have gone abroad, and many of his paintings are of places local to Exeter, like the city itself, the River Exe and Ugbrooke. It was a wash drawing of Ugbrooke, outlined in ink and coloured with a grey and brown wash, which surprised the Sotheby's saleroom on 22 March 2000 by fetching £155 500 against a pre-sale estimate of £25 000 to £35 000.

In 1795 he married Elizabeth Bowling of Pembroke and they had five children; three sons (John, Francis and Arthur who died young) and two daughters (who were unmarried). Francis was Towne's godson. John became rector of Sheepstor from 1831 to 1872, and this would account for the four paintings of the area executed by his father which appear in *The Book of Meavy* by Pauline Hemery (Halsgrove 2000), courtesy of Christies Images Ltd. Until the publication of Pauline Hemery's book it was sometimes stated that John White Abbott was not a Dartmoor artist, but a cluster of his paintings from the Sheepstor area would seem to contradict this. Little research on his life and work has been done. Mallalieu reproduces a John White Abbott picture dated 14 August 1834 in his volume of plates to accompany *The Dictionary of British Watercolour Artists up to 1920*. This one is inscribed 'Leather-Tor from Nanaton [Narrator] Meavy, Devon' and is numbered 26. It is a small picture measuring about 14 x 24cms, of pencil, pen and grey ink and watercolour.

As this book was being written, the Sotheby's sale of 21 March 2001 included 32 of John White Abbott's paintings, including a self-portrait. (These were entered to the sale under the heading 'The Property of a Descendant of the Artist'.) Only three of these were of subjects in the Dartmoor National Park – 'Meavy, Devon', 'The Copper mines on the Dart from Holme [sic] Chase' (not illustrated in the catalogue) and 'Canonteign, Devon'. The last picture, a 30 x 35cm watercolour with pen and grey ink, and executed in 1800 on two sheets of paper joined together, sold for £46 000 – way above the auctioneer's estimate. This was the third highest price in the sale of 398 lots. The highest was £52 000 for a 45 x 57cm John White Abbott watercolour of the lake and trees at Peamore near Exeter.

In 1825 Abbott's uncle James White died, and the nephew inherited the Fordlands estate, just west of Exeter. He retired at this stage to become a country gentleman, and in 1831 was appointed a Deputy Lieutenant for the County of Devon. He was a generous landowner as in *William White's 1850 Directory for Devon*, one year before Abbott died, under 'Public Walks' in the Exeter section one finds the following paragraph:

> *With the permission of the proprietor (J Abbott Esq) many pleasure parties from Exeter often visit Fordlands, near Ide, about 2½ miles west of the city. These romantic grounds from their sylvan shades, gleaming lakes, rustic arbours, and devious, ever-winding paths, might be appropriately denominated*

Fairy-land. The house itself is not a showy mansion, but the grounds are so fancifully laid out, as to attract the attention of numerous visitors. Tea parties are accommodated in the neighbourhood, and numberless are the summer jaunts to this sequestered labyrinth of shady bowers and sylvan walks.

The house was destroyed by fire at the end of the nineteenth century.

It is likely that Abbott, in his declining years, laid out Fordlands to replicate the wooded, well-watered landscapes he had so favoured during his more active painting years at Canonteign, Ugbrooke and Peamore. A 36.8 x 25.4cm watercolour of Fordlands painted in 1842 sold for £900 in the March 2001 Sotheby's sale – less than the estimate.

JOHN WHITE ABBOTT 'Cloth Mill, near Tavistock' June 1824. Pen, ink and watercolour 16 x 22cms.
COURTESY OF RAMM

THOMAS ROWLANDSON Inscribed 'Dartmoor', but known as 'Picnic on Dartmoor'. Watercolour on paper 14.6 x 22.9cms. Another version of this scene called 'An Exmoor Picnic' is illustrated in John Yeates's An Endless View: The Artist and Exmoor *(Exmoor Books 1995).*

COURTESY LEEDS CITY ART GALLERY

Thomas Rowlandson (1756–1827) frequently passed through Devon on his way to visit a friend who lived near Bodmin, and an undated watercolour exists called 'Picnic on Dartmoor'. Rowlandson was always ready to comment in his paintings on human behaviour, and here he places the two servants sitting uncomfortably on a rock, supervising the horses, while two men and two women relax on the grass nearby with their dogs, oblivious of the scenery which they have presumably come to see. The word 'scenery' is itself of interest as, according to the *Oxford English Dictionary*, it came into use in 1784.

Samuel Prout OWS (1783–1852) was one of the first artists to venture on to the high moor, and with his careful and unusual drawings of Dartmoor Prison being constructed in 1807 turned topicality into art. His wash drawings of cottages, mills and bridges – often in a state of decrepitude – and frequently including a peasant in a red jerkin, are statements about the countryside which one feels are not as wildly inaccurate as the efforts of some other practitioners. He became a much sought-after architectural and marine artist, and his works are eminently collectable. Many of his images are reproduced in *Dartmoor Engraved* by Todd Gray.

He was born and educated in Plymouth, and after meeting the antiquary John Britton he was persuaded to move to London, though he returned to Devon and Cornwall from time to time. The bulk of his work, however, was done in Europe.

In Volume 65 of the art magazine *The Connoisseur,* published in 1923, there is an illustrated article by H M Cundall titled, 'Which was the Plagiarist?' in which he comments on the similarity of a painting of Saltram Bridge by Prout with a painting by John Sell Cotman. Clearly, the same shadows, cart with two horses passing the same way over the bridge, and the small boat on the water – these incidents in both pictures – are sufficient to show one painter was a plagiarist. The author, H M Cundall, seems to come down against Cotman.

SAMUEL PROUT 'Dartmoor Prison during construction June 1807'. Graphite and wash 14 x 19cms. Interesting as an example of what we refer to now as 'photo-journalism' (opposite).

COURTESY OF PLYMOUTH CITY MUSEUM & ART GALLERY

'Bennett's Cottage on the Tamar'. Not Dartmoor but nearby. An early work, exhibited at the Royal Academy in 1803. Watercolour, highlighted with gouache, 55 x 67cms.

COURTESY OF RAMM

One of Prout's tutors in Plymouth was **Thomas Hewitt Williams (fl 1800–29)**, a professional artist who travelled around Devon, and crossed into Cornwall and Somerset, producing many pictures which were translated into prints, but these were mostly scenes on the borders of Dartmoor. He also travelled in Wales and exhibited at the Royal Academy between 1801 and 1814. He later moved to Exeter and wrote several guides which he illustrated himself. John Somers Cocks comments in his *Devon Topographical Prints* that Williams 'seems to have spurned the use of a horse on his tours, and thought nothing of walking upwards of 20 miles a day even in bad weather'. His two instructive etchings of Hay Tor Quarry are reproduced in *Dartmoor Engraved* by Todd Gray.

FREDERIC(K) C LEWIS 'Scene from the window of Holne Cottage' 1820, 17 x 24cms. No 9 of a set called 'Scenery of the River Dart'. Aquatint/etching (JVSC 1160).

AUTHOR'S COLLECTION

Frederic(k) Christian Lewis (1779–1856) (there is some doubt about the correct spelling), was born in London and died in Enfield. He came from a well-known family of artists and was primarily an engraver who studied under J C Stadler the German engraver, and at the Royal Academy Schools. However, he came to Devon to pursue his own interests in painting, and as a result he exhibited 56 works in various London galleries, many of them of Dartmoor. Many of his paintings were of river scenes, and he produced several series of etchings and aquatints which involved him in penetrating to the high moor, as Wistman's Wood is represented. Another series included the River Tavy. Several of these are reproduced in *Dartmoor Engraved* by Todd Gray.

Ambrose Bowden Johns (1776–1858) was one of the first Devon-born artists to make his name. He was born in Plymouth and became a bookseller, but soon decided he wanted to be a landscape painter, and built a cottage on the edge of the city. He become friendly with other local artists. He did the statutory painting of Okehampton Castle, and his painting table, which may have been used by Turner, is in the Plymouth Museum & Art Gallery. At least one of his paintings, of Plym Bridge, is in Saltram House.

George Pyne AOWS (1800–84) lived in Tavistock for two years from 1837, and a number of his West Devon pictures were shown at the Royal Watercolour Society exhibitions between 1837 and 1843 when, according to Mallalieu, he retired. He was the son-in-law, until his divorce, of John Varley, and elder son of William Henry Pyne, famous for his *Microcosm (1803–08)*. The Dartmoor paintings George Pyne exhibited were of Peter Tavy Mill, Miners' Cottages at Peter Tavy, Hill Bridge and Brent Tor.

Anthony Vandyke Copley Fielding POWS (1787–1855) is perhaps best known as Copley Fielding, and came from a painting family; his father and four brothers were also artists. He was a pupil of John Varley – see under George Pyne above – and travelled extensively around England, Wales and on the Continent. He showed four paintings with a Dartmoor interest at the exhibitions of the Royal Watercolour Society between 1826 and 1847, but apart from the 'View, near Oakhampton' (sic), they are unspecific as to location. 'Dartmoor, Devon' is not helpful.

Conrad Martens (1801–78) was for a short time a student of Copley Fielding, but is best known as the first landscape artist to make his name in Australia. He has, however, a Dartmoor connection. He was born in London, the youngest of three sons, and when his father died in 1816, the widow, Mrs Rebecca Martens, moved to Exmouth with Conrad. (The author found the grave of Mrs Martens – she died in 1840 – in the churchyard of St John in the Wilderness, Exmouth, in 1995, and removed the lichen which at the time obscured the inscription.)

Conrad Martens had received some painting instruction before leaving London, so kept his hand in by journeying to Plymouth to paint ships, and when he was 21 returned to London, lodged with his next older brother, Henry, and studied landscape painting with Fielding. Among the other artists whose influence he came under were J M W Turner, J S Cotman, Thomas Girtin, David Cox and J R Cozens. Martens was learning his trade in the great age of English watercolour painting and this early contact with these masters was a formative influence when later he was to carry the flag of landscape painting to the infant colony of New South Wales.

Martens was moved by William Gilpin's book *Observations Relative to Picturesque Beauty*. This volume encouraged artists to paint romantic features like ruins, crags and the wilder parts of Britain, and was one of the few books Martens took with him on his one-way journey to Australia.

His Dartmoor expeditions were telescoped into the early 1830s, and his sketchbooks of these trips are in the Dixson Library, Sydney. Some finished pictures are in private collections in England. Because his mother lived in Exmouth many of his subjects were on or near the south coast of Devon and Dorset though he did go north to Exmoor. Among the Dartmoor places he visited and sketched were: the Dewerstone, Tavistock, Buckland Abbey, Chagford, Dunsford, Plym Bridge, Lydford Castle, Ivybridge and High Tor (sic). A 13.3 x 21.6cm watercolour of 'High Tor, Dartmoor' is reproduced in Lionel Lindsay's book about Martens (see Bibliography) and is undoubtedly Hay Tor.

Martens's voyage to Australia is worth remarking upon. He left Plymouth on the *Hyacinth* in the spring of 1833, and reached Rio de Janeiro in July. Here he met a young English officer who was on his way home from Montevideo where his former ship the *Beagle* (Captain Robert FitzRoy) was presently anchored. Charles Darwin, the naturalist, was botanising inland.

This officer, Robert Hamond, told Martens that the ship's artist, Augustus Earle, had been forced to leave the ship through ill health. Martens decided to apply for the job, extracted a reference from the captain of the *Hyacinth*, and made haste to Montevideo. Here he was rowed out to the *Beagle*, applied to Captain FitzRoy for the job of expedition artist, and was duly taken on. A year later, at Valparaiso, Martens himself left the *Beagle*, crossed the Pacific stopping at Tahiti and New Zealand, and eventually reached Sydney in April 1835 where he made his name as the colony's first professional artist.

The visit of **Joseph Mallord William Turner RA (1775–1851)** to Plymouth in the summer of 1813 has been reasonably well documented. Henry Woollcombe, a Plymouth solicitor with a lively interest in art, kept a diary from 1796 to 1828 which is preserved in the Devon Record Office (West Devon). Woollcombe was active in promoting the cultural life of the city, and included the Eastlake family, John Foulston the architect, and Ambrose Johns in his circle. Two fawning entries from Woollcombe's diary establish his grovelling credentials:

> *August 27 Friday morning – Dined at Wm Eastlake's, met a pleasant party, amongst them Mr Turner the Artist whose works I have so much admired, he is brought hither by the beautiful scenery of our neighbourhood, there is a chance of his occasionally residing amongst us, I heartily wish this may take place, as it is always desirable to attract talent around us, where it is accompanied by respectability.*
>
> *Wednesday morning Sept 1st Breakfasted with Mr Turner... had some lively and entertaining conversation, saw all his sketches, with which I was well pleased. Mr Turner is highly pleased with our neighbourhood.*

It has to be said that most of Turner's paintings are not of Dartmoor subjects. He seemed to concentrate more on the immediate vicinity of Plymouth, Plympton and the Hamoaze. However, he did venture up to

J M W TURNER 'Buckfastleigh'. Watercolour on paper c.1826 27.4 x 39.4cms (opposite).
COURTESY OF RAMM

Shaugh Bridge in company with Cyrus Redding, one of the group, who was a journalist in Plymouth. Many years later, in the 1850s, Redding described the time Turner spent in Plymouth. Turner painted Shaugh Bridge which was later destroyed by a flood and subsequently rebuilt. Redding said that he and Turner 'had a picnic on the romantic banks of the Plym, and visited the crags and precipices of Sheeps Tor together'. That is what he wrote, but did he really mean the Dewerstone? He also wrote that this visit 'closed nearly three weeks, for the most part spent in similar rambles'. For part of the time Turner lodged in Ambrose Johns's cottage.

There is an enigmatic reference in one of Turner's 1812/13 sketch books to 'Cranmere Pool'. (See A J Finberg's *A Complete Inventory of Drawings in the Turner Bequest*, two volumes, London 1909, page 373.) The same sketchbook also contains a reference to Dartmeet Bridge, so presumably Turner did penetrate to Dartmoor's higher ground. He exhibited pictures titled 'Near Lustleigh Cleave…' and 'Holm Chase…' at the Royal Watercolour Society exhibitions of 1832 and 1840.

Turner had previously visited Devon – his view of Ivybridge Mill was exhibited at the Royal Academy in 1812. In 1813 he passed through again, and painted the River Erme in quiet mood with a stagecoach being loaded. A hurrying figure crossing the bridge with arm raised adds a touch of Turnerian humour. Did he catch the coach?

In 1826 Turner came to Devon once more and painted Buckfast Abbey looking up the Dart from the hills to the south. This painting was reproduced in *The Perfection of England*, and in his commentary Sam Smiles remarks on the activity in the foreground:

> *The three boys on the left are birdnesting and behind them a shepherd is driving some sheep up the road towards us. Knowing Turner's penchant for symbolic allusions it is tempting to link the boys' robbery and the shorn flock leaving the valley with the predatory dissolution of Buckfast Abbey in 1539 by Henry VIII.*

An anecdote quoted in the pages of *The Western Antiquary* for 1884 Volume 4, page 31 under the heading 'Artists in Devon' touches on Turner's alleged parsimony.

> *Turner, Prout and Varley were on a sketching tour in Devonshire. They had to cross a ferry, the passage-charge for which was twopence. Varley did not happen to have any change, and borrowed the money from Turner – advanced reluctantly. Next morning, Varley and Prout took the Exeter coach for London, leaving Turner behind. But to their surprised gratification, although the hour was daybreak and the morning bleak and dark, they saw Turner at the coach office waiting to see them off. Varley acknowledged the compliment and thanked him. 'No' said Turner, 'it isn't that; but you forgot to give me back the twopence I lent you yesterday.*

This story does not relate which Varley was implicated. Of the two brothers, John and Cornelius, John is known to have executed pictures of Ugbrooke in 1810 and of Torre Abbey and Killerton in 1811, so presumably it was him, the more active painter of the two.

Local artists move on to the moor

The last of Turner's visits to Devon would seem to have drawn a line below the really great names of the artistic establishment for the time being. No truly prominent national figure made a lasting impression on Dartmoor for many years, indeed it appears that the visitors had shown the way, and henceforward it was the home-grown artists who made their mark. With the end of the Napoleonic Wars it was once more possible to travel on the Continent.

Philip Hutchins Rogers (1794–1853) was born in Plymouth and is best known for having drawn and etched the plates for Carrington's *Dartmoor*. He was educated at Plymouth Grammar School under John

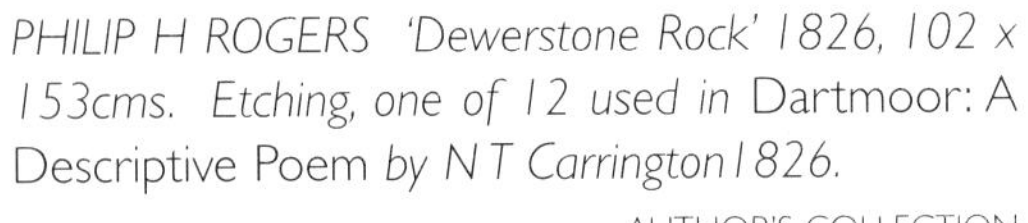

PHILIP H ROGERS 'Dewerstone Rock' 1826, 102 x 153cms. Etching, one of 12 used in Dartmoor: A Descriptive Poem *by N T Carrington1826.*
AUTHOR'S COLLECTION

Bidlake, who recognised his talent and paid for him to study in London. He frequently returned to Devon painting rural and marine topics, mostly in oil. Apart from his Carrington commission he did not paint many Dartmoor subjects, though his oil 'A Scene on the Commons of Dartmoor – Noon' was exhibited and illustrated in the catalogue of the spring 2000 sale of J Collins & Son of Bideford. (A larger oil of Lympstone was in the same exhibition.) He was a highly competent artist and sold most of his pictures in London. The London exhibition catalogues show 85 of his paintings in forty-three years. He travelled a good deal on the Continent, and spent his last years in Germany, where he died near Baden-Baden, having originally gone there 'from motives of economy'. His pictures may be seen in Plymouth Museum & Art Gallery and at Saltram House.

PHILIP H ROGERS 'A Scene on the Commons of Devon – Noon'. Oil on canvas 33 x 44.5cms. Probably c.1820, priced at £10 10s including the frame. Site of the subject unknown; may be in the Two Bridges area.

COURTESY J COLLINS & SON

Not much is known about **Francis Stevens OWS (1781–1822 or 1823)**. He seems to have settled in Exeter in 1817 as a drawing master, having already exhibited in London and Norwich. In 1820 he gave an oil painting to the Devon & Exeter Institution where it hangs over the fireplace, and is probably one of the first large paintings of Dartmoor proper. It is appropriate it hangs where it does, as Stevens died not long after 'having fallen down in apoplexy at the door of the Devon & Exeter Institution', as George Pycroft wrote in *Art in Devonshire* (Eland 1883).

FRANCIS STEVENS 'Lustleigh Cleave' 1820. Oil on canvas 145 x 194cms.

COURTESY OF DEVON & EXETER INSTITUTION

John Frederick Lewis RA POWS (1805–76) visited Devon in 1829, and his work is illustrated in *The Perfection of England* where the relationships of the various members of the Lewis clan are also unravelled. He stayed with the Reverend and Mrs Bray while in West Devon.

John Glover (1767–1849) was an art teacher who was highly successful, and acquired the *soubriquet* the 'English Claude'. He is credited with inventing split brushwork, to paint foliage quickly and accurately. He painted his watercolour of 'The Teign near Drewsteignton, Devonshire' in 1829, but otherwise he is not known as a Dartmoor artist. This picture is illustrated in *The Perfection of England*, and is painted from Prestonbury looking down on Fingle Bridge and Fingle Mill. Drewsteignton is just visible on the right. The picture is almost an air photograph in its grey-green tint hinting at monochrome, and the high vantage point of the artist. He emigrated to Tasmania in 1831 with his family, and his work there is highly regarded.

Edward Duncan RWS (1803–82) was a versatile London-based artist who painted several different subjects – landscape, marine, genre and architectural. He usually worked in watercolour, but he was also a lithographer and aquatinter. He went on numerous sketching tours, and his only qualification for listing here is two entries in a list of works exhibited by Duncan at the New Society of Painters in Water-Colours, the Gallery, Exeter Hall, Strand, London in 1837. These are 'Sketch from Nature, Dartmoor, Devon' and 'Dartmoor, from the Newton Road'. (*The Old Water-Colour Society's Club*, 60th annual volume, Adrian Bury, editor, 1985.)

John Skinner Prout NWS (1806–76) was a nephew of Samuel Prout. Like his uncle, he was born in Plymouth, but moved to Bristol and later emigrated temporarily to Australia. His study of the ever popular Ivybridge, executed in July 1836, is illustrated in *The Perfection of England*, and he also did one of Sheepstor a few days earlier.

WILLIAM SPREAT 'Viaduct over the valley of the Erme at Ivy Bridge' 1848 29 x 51cms (JVSC 1373). Lithograph by Spreat after a watercolour by William Dawson. No 5 in a set of six called 'Six sketches illustrative of the South Devon Railway'.

AUTHOR'S COLLECTION

William Spreat (1816–still alive 1889) was born in Exeter, and by the 1840s was an artist and lithographer, publisher and printer. He is probably best known for his *Picturesque Sketches of the Churches of Devon* (1842), some of which are Dartmoor scenes. Two years later a folio of 12 lithographs with descriptive text titled *River Scenery of Devon 1st Series, The Teign* appeared, followed in about 1845 by *Dartmoor and its Borders*, an eight-lithograph set of the area around Hay Tor. Despite being described as '1st Series', Spreat's Teign set was the only one he completed of the river scenery of Devon. John Somers Cocks in his Introduction to *Devon Topographical Prints* writes at length about Spreat's artistic and publishing enterprises.

William Dawson (1789–after 1865) was an Exeter civil engineer who is chiefly remembered for the paintings from which William Spreat produced the lithographs for the set of prints entitled 'Six sketches illustrative of the South Devon Railway' 1848. No 6 in this series is of the Slade Viaduct, and appears on the dust-jacket of *Devon Topographical Prints* by John Somers Cocks.

Henry Bright (1810–73) was represented in *The Perfection of England* by a c.1840 pencil and watercolour picture 'On the borders of Dartmoor'. It shows a woman and child walking towards the artist, and passing a ramshackle mill with overshot waterwheel. Dartmoor looms on the horizon with Lydford Church and Castle in the middle-distance. Bright was a member of the Norwich School of painters and he worked in coloured chalk as well as oil and watercolour. He lived in London for twenty years, where he was an art teacher. A painting by Bright of the ruins of St Benedict's Abbey in Norfolk was acquired by Samuel Prout whose son remembered that the painting 'so much delighted my father… that he gave the artist, then a young man, one of his drawings in exchange for it.'

HENRY BRIGHT 'On the Borders of Dartmoor' c.1840. Watercolour 45.6 x 75.9cms.
NORWICH CASTLE MUSEUM & ART GALLERY

JOHN MIDDLETON 'Sunshine and shade, Ivy Bridge'. Watercolour 32.9 x 48.5cms.
NORWICH CASTLE MUSEUM & ART GALLERY

John Middleton (1827–56) was a pupil in Norwich of Henry Bright whose fresh, direct style of sketching from nature brought him early recognition from the art press of the day. It seems also to have prompted his teacher to make his own studies less contrived on their sketching expeditions. It is not known when his trip(s) to Devon took place. He was also a keen photographer and his watercolour of a boulder-strewn river bed with dappled light filtering through at Ivybridge was the kind of subject very much in vogue with photographers and artists alike in the 1850s. Sadly, his promising career was cut short at the age of 29 from consumption.

John Gendall (1789–1865) is sometimes referred to as 'Exeter's forgotten artist'. This is partly his own fault, as he rarely signed his pictures. But for some reason his work was forgotten after his death and present-day researchers have had to dig deep to make sense of his life's activities. He was brought up on Exe Island, near Exe Bridge, and became the servant of James White in Friars Walk. White was the uncle of John White Abbott, another Exeter-born artist, who was a friend of Francis Towne. Gendall thus came into early contact with the local artistic community. Early in life he became friendly with William Traies, who also became a painter, and they made sketching tours of the countryside near Exeter. They were both born in the same year.

A representative of the London art firm of Ackermann's happened to see one of Gendall's drawings in the Exeter shop owned by Charles Cole, and in 1811 White encouraged his protégé to go to London to widen his horizons. He performed a variety of tasks for Ackermanns, some of which led to publications. Then from 1819 to 1825 he travelled all over England, into Scotland and across to France. We know he painted Great Fulford in 1826 from across the lake as the aquatint derived from this picture is reproduced in *Devon Country Houses and Gardens Engraved* by Todd Gray, 2001.

About this time Gendall returned to Exeter, and went into partnership with his old friend Cole, though this was later dissolved, when Gendall took over what we know as Mol's Coffee House as a picture-framing and art-school business. In the mid-1840s one finds him painting on the edge of Dartmoor, his favourite spots being the Avon near South Brent, Chagford and Chudleigh. These pictures were often river subjects. 'Scenes on the Avon, Dartmoor' was exhibited at the Royal Academy and other acceptances followed.

In the 1860s he was a founder member of the Devonshire Association, and in the same decade Gendall supported the move to build a museum with room for a school of art, in memory of Prince Albert. Glendall died three years before the museum opened in 1868.

Jane Baker, formerly Curator of Fine Art at the Royal Albert Memorial Museum has written of Gendall's work.

> *At their best, Gendall's paintings rise well above the level generally found in the work of a competent provincial landscape painter. This is usually seen in his watercolours, in which, at times, he achieved the luminosity of colour and vibrant atmosphere one usually associates with artists of the calibre of J M W Turner or the French Impressionist School.*

It is likely his name was pronounced with a soft 'G'.

William Traies (1789–1872) was born in Crediton the same year as John Gendall, and decided when quite young to be an artist. He appears to have moved to Exeter to find work, and his artistic talent was recognised by the Reverend Gayer Patch, the vicar of St Leonard's parish in the city, who possessed a large collection of watercolours.

Patch introduced Traies to Joseph Farington RA, who we have come across previously, when the latter visited Exeter in 1810, and Farington noted the occasion in his diary, though he appears not to have shared Patch's opinion.

> *After tea a young man of the name of Traile (sic) came, it being the wish of Mr Patch that I should see him as his mind is bent upon being an artist. I looked at a few of his attempts at drawing and found he had everything to learn; but his resolution seemed to be fixed. He told me he was twenty-one years old, and at present employed as a Clerk to a manufacturer… I remarked that he had but one eye but was informed it was not due to any weakness in those parts but that he was born so, and saw well with the other.*

Patch, still anxious to get Traies started, now introduced him to a clerical colleague, the Reverend Palk Carrington, Rector of Bridford in the Teign valley, and here the artist spent a good deal of time. He exhibited several paintings at the Royal Academy, including one titled 'Waterfall on the Teign, near Lustleigh, Devon'. Traies's patrons now included Captain Parker of Whiteway House, Chudleigh, the father of the MP for South Devon, and the painter was able to keep a studio there.

He married the daughter of John Downman, the miniaturist, at Holy Trinity Church, Exeter, in 1825, and they had three sons. The second, variously known as **John Francis, Francis, Frank** or **Frank Downman Traies (1828–57)**, himself became an artist, though his early death meant he never developed his full potential. He was, however, able to complete a large oil now at the RAMM called 'Landscape with figures and animals – collecting heather' dated 1852. (The author has leaned on Bill Ransom's researches – see Bibliography – in regard to Traies junior's dates and details.)

FRANCIS D TRAIES 'Landscape with figures and animals – collecting heather' 1852. Oil on canvas 45 x 73cms. Heather was used for a variety of purposes on Dartmoor farms – animal bedding, firing an oven, and even as a thatching material.

COURTESY OF RAMM

Traies senior continued painting, and most of his work ended up on the walls of local gentry. When he painted in what we now call the Dartmoor National Park the subjects were on the eastern borders – places like Fingle Bridge, Holy Street Mill (Chagford), and Bridford. Like John Glover he was given the more localised *soubriquet* the 'Devonshire Claude', but while his paintings may suggest the Continental master, it is more likely his model was Richard Wilson. His river scenes often include the dead branch of a tree sticking out of the water.

William Traies latterly lived at Parkers' Well Cottage, Topsham Road, Exeter, near St Leonard's Church, and here he died in April 1872.

James Leakey (1775–1865) is not known as a Dartmoor artist, but as he painted Devon landscapes, and was 90 when he died, a Dartmoor painting may yet turn up, so we have included him here. At the 1973 exhibition *The Devonshire Scene* at the Royal Albert Memorial Museum there were 13 Leakey paintings on view, none of them moorland subjects, though several were of the River Dart below Totnes. He was a versatile painter, quite able to turn his hand to miniatures, portraits and genre subjects. He was born and died in Exeter, but spent some time in London about the middle of his life. He painted the portrait of John White Abbott reproduced on page 22.

Peter de Wint OWS (1784–1849), the well-established London drawing master, and the son of a Dutch-American father and a Scottish mother, came to Devon the year before he died, and painted near Holne Bridge while staying with the Champernownes at Dartington Hall. At the Fitzwilliam Museum, Cambridge, there is a watercolour which shows a view looking up the Dart towards Holne Bridge with a mill on the left, cows standing in the water, and a fisherman on the bank.

PETER DE WINT 'On the Dart'. Watercolour 55.8 x 93cms.

COURTESY FITZWILLIAM MUSEUM, CAMBRIDGE

Charles Frederick Williams (fl 1841–81) is best remembered for his set of ten drawings produced for the first edition of the Reverend Samuel Rowe's *A Perambulation of the Antient and Royal Forest of Dartmoor* (1848), lithographed by Paul Gauci, a London-based practitioner. Williams was an Exeter drawing master, so it is not surprising that the ten illustrations have a tendency towards eastern Dartmoor. His selection of sites – Scorhill Circle, Grimspound, Postbridge clapper bridge, and the Tolmen on the North Teign saved on travel when getting around was still difficult. We know he painted in oil and watercolour, and did other print sets outside Dartmoor, also with Gauci, but little else is recorded about this artist.

The paintings of **John Wallace Tucker (1808–69)** have become very sought-after. He was born in Exeter, and seems to have lived there all his life, at various addresses: Bartholomew Yard, Mint Lane and Alphington Road.

His range of country was west to the Tamar, north to Lynton and many places in between, and he was not concerned with painting such unfashionable locations as Lapford, Landkey lime kilns, and Ogwell, frequently choosing a subject with a rustic footbridge. Four of the 23 paintings by J W Tucker on view at *The Devonshire Scene* exhibition of 1973 had rustic footbridges in them, and others were of stone bridges and Tarr Steps on Exmoor. His pictures give a good sense of rural Devon, if a somewhat romantic view of life in the mid-nineteenth century. His Dartmoor territory tended to be the Teign and Bovey valleys, though a small 10 x 15cm painting 'Between Sticklepath and Okehampton' is known. He painted for about forty years, and died at his home in the Mint, Exeter.

Frederick Richard Lee RA (1798–1879) was born and spent much of his life in Barnstaple. As a young man he joined the army, and saw service in the Low Countries, but became a student at the Royal Academy Schools, four years later exhibiting his first-known picture – of Lynmouth – at the British Institution. By 1838 he was a full Academician. He is not known as a Dartmoor artist, though Peter Howard in his PhD thesis (see Bibliography) states that he painted on the River Tavy. One rarely sees his paintings at local auctions.

An oil by Lee painted in 1842 is reproduced in John Yeates's *An Endless View: The Artist and Exmoor* (Exmoor Books 1995). Although simply captioned 'Devonshire Scenery' the picture is of a watermill in a Dartmoor-type landscape with hills rising steeply on both sides. Holy Street Mill at Chagford could well have been the subject for this picture, though, if so, the elements have been somewhat rejigged. The same picture appears in Christopher Wood's *Paradise Lost: Paintings of English Country Life and Landscape 1850–1914* (Past Times 1997).

Benjamin Disraeli (1804–81), the Tory politician and Prime Minister, who became the Earl of Beaconsfield, wrote several powerful and successful novels, and in his *Coningsby* (1844) his industrialist character Mr Millbank remarks that he prefers 'a fine free landscape by Lee, that gave him the broad plains, the green lanes, and running streams of his own land'. The Lee he was referring to was F R Lee. Thackeray was another writer to refer to Lee, in an article in *Fraser's Magazine* for July 1840.

Sailing in due course became his main interest, and he cruised in the Baltic and the Mediterranean either in his own yacht or in one belonging to a friend. He sometimes combined sailing with painting, but towards the end of his life gave up painting, went to South Africa, and died there in Cape Colony.

Thomas Mogford (1809–68) was born in Exeter the son of a veterinary surgeon. He studied art under Gendall and Cole, whose daughter he married, and they lived in Northernhay Place, later moving to London. He was both a portrait and landscape painter, and for a time exhibited annually at the Royal Academy. From 1848 he visited Exeter annually to paint portraits and frequently rented 'some humble cottage-lodging on Dartmoor' (as Pycroft wrote) to build up a body of sketches to work on later. His pictures are rarely seen at local auctions. Towards the end of his life he spent much time in Guernsey, where he died aged 59. His self-portrait may be seen in the front office of the Devon & Exeter Institution.

It is temping to attribute the discovery of new landscapes by artists to the arrival of the railways, but North Wales and the Lake District had been popular before the railways reached these relatively remote areas. The railway was but one factor among many – though an important one – which led to the opening up of the British countryside.

A milestone at the half-way point in the century was the publication in 1850 of the first edition of Murray's *Handbook for Travellers in Devon and Cornwall*. This went into at least 11 editions (up to 1895), and the fourth edition (1859) was reissued in facsimile in 1971 by David & Charles. This was the first cheap reliable guidebook for the two counties, and was recommended to artists by no less a painter than **Samuel Palmer RWS (1805–81)** who wrote, 'It was written by an artist and has a real savour of Devonshire perception, which will be found very rare.' He wrote this in a letter in 1865, for by this time he had made four visits to Devon, though Dartmoor was only one of the visually-attractive places he visited in the county, Clovelly and Lynton being others. He also painted Tintagel (Cornwall) and Culbone (Somerset). In another letter he referred to 'dear spongy Devon'.

He had painted Chudleigh Rocks as early as 1834, though this painting seems to be lost. The *Catalogue Raisonné of the Works of Samuel Palmer* by Raymond Lister (Cambridge 1988) is useful for tracking down his works. Palmer was in Devon in 1858, the year Donati's Comet was visible, for he painted a watercolour, now in a private collection, titled 'The Comet of 1858, as seen from the Skirts of Dartmoor'.

Eleven years later, he used his memories and sketches of Dartmoor as he worked on his imagined landscapes inspired by Milton and Virgil. He was particularly proud of one painting, now in a private collection, a watercolour with body colour, which was done to illustrate Milton's *Il Penseroso*. This was 'Morning' or 'The Dripping Eaves' and he wrote, 'Rightly or wrongly, I fancy that the dark moorland is the best thing I have ever done. I aimed at Southern Dartmoor sentiment where the valleys run with cream and where they clout pilchard pies with clotted cream.'

In another letter he referred to '...rich glebes such as adorn the sides of Dartmoor', but such references as have survived relate to the moorland borders. We have seen that Palmer painted Chudleigh Rocks in 1834. In 1866 he wrote about it in a letter, quoted in *The Letters of Samuel Palmer* (Raymond Lister, edit, Clarendon Press 1974):

> *Worth seeing, if you don't stop short as the tourists do, on the wrong side of the chasm gaping at the opposite cliff – while the real spectacle is what they are standing upon. I found it all strewed with picnic bottles and broken plates.*

Clearly, litter is not a modern phenomenon.

Edward Lear (1812–88) is best known for his nonsense verse, but he was an able self-taught artist who is included in this book on the evidence of Charles Hartley (later Sir Charles Hartley KCMG FRSE 1825–1915) who was in mid-century resident engineer for the civil engineering works at Sutton Harbour, Plymouth. A paper summarising Charles Hartley's diaries was published in the *Transactions* of the Devonshire Association for 1983 (Vol 115) and includes some details of an encounter with Edward Lear on Dartmoor in 1851.

Lear had been born in London, the 20th child in a family of 21 siblings, and had become an ornithological draughtsman for the Zoological Society. He later entered the employ of the Earl of Derby from 1832–36, but in 1837 began his travels as a topographical painter which continued for forty years, diligently recording his wanderings in distinctive and highly competent colour-washed drawings which he worked up into saleable paintings to finance further travels.

Among the places he visited were Italy, Greece, Palestine, Egypt, Switzerland, Malta and France, and towards the end of his life he travelled extensively in India and Ceylon. He died at his home in San Remo. Lear was based in London from 1850–54, and it was in 1851 that he met Hartley by chance in Chagford. Hartley was only 26, and had walked to Chagford from South Brent.

> *Together they walked to Whiddon Park and Manaton, bathed in Widecombe brook* (sic) *and put up for the night at Two Bridges. The next three days were spent walking and sketching together on the fringe of Dartmoor and they then returned together to Plymouth. Lear was just publishing his volume of* Journals of a Landscape Painter in Greece and Albania*, and his travels through Italy and south-eastern Europe fascinated Hartley; and their close companionship in this short excursion illustrates the 'genius for friendship' with which Lear is credited. He was full of stories and riddles some of which Hartley noted down. They talked to the labourers and countrywomen whom they met on the way. Most had never seen the sea.*

A comprehensive exhibition of Lear's paintings, and some surviving memorabilia, was staged at the Royal Academy in 1985, and the author has seen the catalogue compiled by Vivien Noakes. Likewise, the 1995 biography by Peter Levi, *Edward Lear: A Biography* has been scanned, but no reference to Lear's 1851 walking tour has been found in either publication. Perhaps something will turn up one day.

John William Inchbold (1830–88) was a landscape painter in the Pre-Raphaelite circle, and a protégé of Ruskin. So far as Dartmoor is concerned his most important contribution is an oil titled 'The Moorland (Dewer-Stone, Dartmoor)' and is dated 1854. This picture is drawn from the opposite side of the Plym valley to the Dewerstone, looking westwards, with a sky lit by the setting sun. A crow enlivens the foreground. The picture is illustrated in *The Perfection of England* (plate 33) and in a larger format on page 16/17 of *The British Landscape: Through the eyes of the Great Artists* by Richard Humphreys (Hamlyn/Tate Gallery 1990). It is owned by the Tate Gallery. Later in the 1850s he painted an oil 'Furze blossom from Devonshire' and an oil and a watercolour of 'Cornwood', both in 1860. He also painted extensively in the mountains of Austria, Germany and Switzerland.

Benjamin W Leader RA (1831–1923) was born into a family called Williams, but he changed his name when he was about 26 as there were so many other artists called Williams – see *post.* (He was not from the same Williams family as produced H J Boddington and S R Percy.)

Leader was born in Worcester, and was destined to be a civil engineer, like his father, but Benjamin was determined to be an artist, so studied in his spare time at the Worcester School of Design before being admitted to the Royal Academy Schools.

We are fortunate to have a comprehensive monograph about the artist written by Ruth Wood, published by the Antique Collectors' Club in 1998, and called *Benjamin Williams Leader RA 1831–1923 His Life and Paintings.* This informs us that he visited Scotland in the 1850s, also Surrey and later North Wales, which became a favourite sketching area. He often travelled and worked with a friend, another landscape artist, George Vicat Cole.

Ruth Wood tells us that Leader had been courting Mary Eastlake, a great-niece of Sir Charles Lock Eastlake, President of the Royal Academy from 1850 until his death in 1865. She lived at Horrabridge, on the edge of Dartmoor. This ties in with William Crossing's remarks in his article 'The Artist', written in the *Western Morning News* in 1903 and republished in 1966 in a book called *Crossing's Dartmoor Worker*, still in print. Crossing wrote:

> *Painted on the shutters in a room in the Duchy Hotel at Princetown are some exquisite little gems. I have seen it stated that one of them is by Mr B W Leader, whose brush has so ably depicted Dartmoor, but Mr Aaron Rowe* (then landlord of the hotel, now the High Moorland Visitor Centre) *informs me that he believes it is the work of Mr A B Collier, who painted it when staying at the hotel some thirty or forty years ago with Mr Leader.*

Benjamin and Mary were married in 1876 at Buckland Monachorum when he was 45 and she 23. Their honeymoon lasted three months, and after a few days in Cornwall they went to Worcestershire, London, Paris and Switzerland. Benjamin was later able to use his Continental sketches to work up a number of Swiss scenes.

During his long life Leader exhibited 216 paintings at the Royal Academy from 1854, but it was his dour and highly atmospheric 1881 painting 'February Fill Dyke' of a humble cottage at sunset, with the light of the sky reflected in the waterlogged track along which some figures are trudging, which made his reputation. The Leaders moved to Surrey from Worcester in 1889 and stayed there for the rest of their lives. Mary lived until 1938.

Despite Crossing's comment that Leader's 'brush has so ably depicted Dartmoor' few of his local works seem to have survived or are known of. Ruth Wood's book contains colour reproductions of two, 'A Fine Day on Dartmoor' (1878) and 'On the Borders of Dartmoor' (1881). Neither are identifiable, though both show a broad sweep of moorland, with some human interest, and the latter shows a settlement and something which could be an engine house. Both were done at the peak of his 'February Fill Dyke' powers.

In her recent memoire *A House Unlocked* (Viking 2001) Penelope Lively has written about a Leader picture which used to hang in the dining-room of Golsoncott, the country house in West Somerset where she spent so much time as a girl. She refers to it as the 'Sunset Painting', and for her, from the age of 14 through to about 17, it expressed everything she felt about the country.

Edmund Morison Wimperis VPRI (1835–1900) painted in oil and watercolour, and his works fetch good prices on the rare occasions they come on the market. In his life he exhibited widely. He was born in Chester, learned the trade of wood engraver, then moved to the *Illustrated London News* and other magazines. He studied under Myles Birket Foster, and made friends with another well-known painter, Thomas Collier – who is not understood to have a Dartmoor connection – and painted extensively. Whether he had a local base in Devon is not known, though William Crossing wrote about him in the chapter 'The Artist' in *Crossing's Dartmoor Worker* (1903):

> *Although the majority of our Dartmoor painters depict the moor in its summer dress, I cannot but think that the late E M Wimperis, sometime Vice President of the Royal Institute of Painters in Watercolours, was right when he said that it did not look so well in sunshine as when the mist wreaths hung about its tors. Faithful to his convictions he has given us many fine pictures of the moor when the rain is beating its sides, or when eddying mists half shroud the hills. Dartmoor at such time looks grand and mysterious, and if its spirit can then be caught the effect is wonderfully striking. But this cannot always be done; the artist perhaps is not on the spot. Naturally he loves the fine weather, and does not turn his attention to Dartmoor when the cloud bursts upon it, and yet Mr Wimperis said that the most valuable notes he had ever taken in his life was when he was wrapped up in a mackintosh; he did not believe, he said, in being a fine-weather artist.*

A painting by Wimperis, 'Mists lifting off Dartmoor', an oil on canvas dated 1897, is a fine example of an upland view. It could have been painted on Taw Marsh, looking south with the mist rising on the slopes to the west. Some cattle and the river enliven the foreground. It was reproduced in colour in J Collins & Son's catalogue for their spring exhibition of 1996.

EDMUND M WIMPERIS 'Mists lifting off Dartmoor'. Oil on canvas 61 x 91.5cms (right).

COURTESY OF J COLLINS & SON

'Mists lifting off Dartmoor'. Sepia postcard. Similar to the painting featured right, but with sheep in the foreground.

AUTHOR'S COLLECTION

Philip Mitchell RI (1814–96) was born in Devonport and at 14 moved to Falmouth. It is possible he served in the Royal Navy, but in 1845, by now a self-taught artist, we know he settled in Plymouth and became a member of Plymouth Sketching Club which included Ambrose Johns. He did not travel much, though a picture of his of the Lake District is known.

An 1853 peaceful, well-painted watercolour by Mitchell which is probably located on the edge of Dartmoor was illustrated in colour in J Collins & Son's catalogue for June 1999 entitled 'A Devonshire wooded river landscape with cattle watering while a drover sits on a rock beside'. Other paintings of his the author has seen tend to be of West Devon, and particularly of the River Tavy.

The second half of the nineteenth century saw the establishment of a number of substantial art magazines: *The Art Journal, The Magazine of Art* and *The Portfolio*. It became quite usual for artists having discovered an area they regarded as visually attractive, to dash off an article for fellow painters extolling its merits. In 1880 Professor D T Ansted FRS wrote an article in *The Art Journal* called 'Sources and Early Courses of Rivers in Granite'. He wrote, 'Dartmoor is, however, well worthy of the attention of those artists who love the grotesque as well as the monotonous in nature.'

J Arthur Blaikie wrote three articles in *The Magazine of Art* in 1885 about the lower reaches of 'The Dart'. The third and last covered the stretch from Buckfastleigh up to New Bridge. Blaikie also wrote in *The Art Journal* in the same year under the heading 'On Dartmoor'. Here he concentrated on Ashburton, Widecombe-in-the-Moor and Chagford.

J L W Page is best known as the author of *An Exploration of Dartmoor…* (Seeley & Co, first edition 1889), but he had four articles published in *The Portfolio* of that year previewing his book. Seeley & Co also published *The Portfolio*! Again in 1893 he trailered his *Rivers of Devon* (Seeley & Co 1893) by writing four articles in *The Portfolio*. All these articles were illustrated by pictures drawn by Page and Alfred Dawson.

Artists had now been painting Dartmoor long enough for some landscape preferences to become discernible. The ideal composition was a view looking up a boulder-strewn river. Looking up was eminently preferable to looking down, as falls and cataracts appeared more animated. The valley sides should slope steeply down, and if possible be broken by crags and rocks, and be clothed by heather in bloom. Near the foot of the slope there should be a few trees. If a small bridge, cottage, or, best of all, a watermill with working overshot waterwheel could be introduced without cluttering the scene overmuch, then perfection could be achieved, not forgetting, of course, the little man in a red coat. Some artists regarded the representation of Dartmoor tors, rocks and boulders, with their appropriate light, shade and a patina of lichen, as a challenge to their skill akin to life drawing.

The popularity of Okehampton Castle and Ivybridge has already been mentioned. Bickleigh Vale, Shaugh Bridge, Lydford Gorge and Holy Street Mill (Chagford) are other sites which were regularly portrayed. All are on the edge of the moor, the first two near Plymouth. Holy Street Mill was easily accessible from Chagford which in the second half of the nineteenth century developed as a holiday centre. If Bickleigh Vale is near Plymouth, some 40 miles away in the east of Devon is another Bickleigh, also with a bridge and on the River Exe. Artists, not known for accuracy of the captions to their paintings, were frequently guilty of painting this Bickleigh and mis-titling their efforts as 'Bickleigh Vale'.

J L W Page in his *An Exploration of Dartmoor* mentioned above – and indeed in the article he wrote in *The Portfolio* advertising this book – wrote of Holy Street Mill as follows:

> *Of the many interesting and beautiful spots in the vicinity, we can only make passing mention. None will be allowed to remain long in the town without hearing of Holy Street Mill – the 'grist mill' as it is commonly called – an old thatched watermill by the Teign, beloved by artists for generations...*

It is perhaps more interesting to note what was *not* considered worth immortalising in art. Mines – and there were a number operating on the moor – were hardly ever represented, though a few quarries were painted: Cann Quarry, handy to Plymouth, and the Hay Tor Quarries with the granite tramway were occasional subjects. From the catalogue of *Devon Topographical Prints* it can be seen that no prints exist for the parishes of North Bovey, Throwleigh, Belstone and Sourton.

An early colour postcard, posted in 1904. The caption reads 'An Old Mill on Dartmoor', and it is probably Holy Street Mill, Chagford, a favourite subject for artists in the nineteenth century.

AUTHOR'S COLLECTION

The Dartmoor painting families

During the middle and later years of the nineteenth century several families become known as painters of Dartmoor. The Williams family of London were the visitors to the moor. The other family groups, the Widgerys, Brittans, Morrishs and Sherrins, were local to Devon.

We are fortunate that Jan Reynolds researched and wrote a book in 1975 called *The Williams Family of Painters* which disentangles the complicated relationships and lists many of the landscape works produced by members of the family. An oil painting titled 'The Vale of Ashburton, South Devon', signed and dated 1844, sold at Sotheby's in March 2001 for £32 000. It was by **Henry John Boddington (1811–1865)**, one of the Williams family of artists. The view appears to be looking up a low-running River Dart towards Holne Bridge. Some cattle are drinking, a man sits astride a white horse, and several people are sitting on the river bank.

Boddington was the second son of Edward Williams who had five other sons, all of whom became artists specialising in the same field, and some of them came to Dartmoor also. Being born Henry John Williams he adopted his wife's name – she was Clare Boddington – to distinguish himself and avoid confusion.

In addition to Boddington's 'Vale of Ashburton' we find from Jan Reynolds's book that he painted two pictures in 1843 titled 'On the Webber, South Devon' and 'On the River Webber'. These must surely refer to the Webburn river which flows into the Dart a few miles upstream from Holne Bridge. The author remarks that the artists' 'versions of place-names, in general, are decidedly unreliable'. (This fault is not confined to the Williams family.) Boddington also exhibited a painting in 1847 titled 'Watermill near the Moor, Devonshire'.

Apart from visiting the west of England, this London-based artist painted in Scotland, Wales, Yorkshire and Derbyshire. His pictures are usually signed to include his second initial. Those simply signed 'Boddington' are by his son Edwin. There was an unrelated Henry Boddington who painted as a gifted amateur and paintings signed 'H Boddington' or 'Henry Boddington' are probably from the brush of this artist.

Ruskin praised his paintings for their honesty, and for their obvious love of the countryside. A fondness for the style of Constable may be seen, but his eyesight began to fail in early middle age, and he died of a progressive brain disease.

The fifth of the six brothers, **Sidney Richard Percy Williams (1821–1886)** has become the most fashionable painter in the family. He dropped his surname to be known as **S R Percy**, and painted in the same part of Dartmoor, at the same time, the mid-1840s, as his brother Henry. Perhaps they travelled together. He even mis-captioned an 1843 picture 'Sheep washing on the Webber' in the same way. Other pictures known are 'A Lane in Holne Chase, South Devon' (exhibited at the Royal Academy in 1843) and 'Twilight on the Dart – moon rising'. He also painted in Switzerland, Italy, Wales, Scotland, the Isle of Wight and the Lake District. He had a grandson who became a pupil of Stanhope Forbes RA in Cornwall, but who was killed on 2 October 1918, just weeks before the end of the First World War.

Jan Reynolds comments in her book that of all the Williams family he was the artist who adjusted the scenery most to suit what he felt should be seen. He also used a camera to freeze the moment for later use in the studio.

The youngest brother **Alfred Walter Williams (1824–1905)** was always close to his brother Sidney, and is known to have painted 'Buckfastleigh, Devon' and 'A Lane near Ashburton, Devon', the latter in 1845. He also painted in Switzerland, Italy, Wales, Scotland, Jersey, Cornwall, Exmoor and on the Thames.

The last of this Williams family to paint on Dartmoor was the son of George Augustus Williams (1814–1901) who is not known for any local connection. He was **Walter Williams (1835–1906)**, and his picture 'A July study of Devonshire wild flowers with Dartmoor hills in the distance' was exhibited at the Royal Academy in 1859. Another picture called 'Early morning on Dartmoor' is known from 1874. He also painted in North Devon, Essex, Yorkshire and Wales.

'Portrait of William Widgery' by his son, F J Widgery c.1887. Oil on canvas 91 x 71cms.

COURTESY OF RAMM

Ask someone at the present time to name a Dartmoor artist, and it may be difficult to get a response, or could depend on where they live. The Widgerys, William and F J, father and son, because they were based in Exeter – though William lived for several years at Lydford – are remembered on the east of the moor and along the north-west side, and are well represented in the Exeter art collection at the Royal Albert Memorial Museum.

On the south-west fringe of the moor and around Tavistock we find the two Brittans, confusingly both Charles E, father and son, are more to the fore as they lived and worked in that part of Devon.

The other clan to be remembered as Dartmoor artists were the several members of the Morrish family who made Chagford their base, and whose paintings come on the market with some regularity.

Yet more father-and-son artists who made their mark were George Henry Jenkins and his son of the same name, the Sherrins, Daniel and Reginald Daniel, and William Williams and his son Roscoe. Between them these artists have made a considerable impact on the Dartmoor scene.

It was in the late 1850s that the paintings of **William Widgery (1826–93)** first began to influence public taste. His younger son **Frederick John Widgery (1861–1942)** inherited his father's artistic talent, and was already turning out respectable work by 1883 (*Art in Devonshire*, Pycroft 1883). As F J Widgery was painting until the late 1930s the Widgery span of influence covers nearly seventy years.

WILLIAM WIDGERY 'The Expanse of the Moor'. Oil on canvas 23 x 122cms (above).

COURTESY J COLLINS & SON

'Fingle Bridge'. Oil on canvas.

COURTESY OF RAMM

William Widgery was born in North Molton among the southern foothills of Exmoor in humble circumstances. (Until recently it was thought he was born in 1822, but a baptismal entry seems to confirm 1826 as the correct date.) Trained as a mason, he came to Exeter as a young man, and quickly took up painting in his spare time. He received no formal training, and learned his art by copying the work of others. He soon set up his own studio and began to travel. Dartmoor was his first love, but he went to Italy and Switzerland twice, to Venice, and painted the coast of Devon and Cornwall. By 1883, Pycroft wrote that William Widgery had 'painted over 3000 pictures, and has sold them all; indeed, they are generally sold before they are off his easel'.

William loved western Dartmoor and had a house built at Lydford in 1880 between what is now the A386 and the village, which at the present time – somewhat altered – is the Lydford House Hotel, where he lived for ten years. He painted in oils and watercolours, and occasionally turned to portrait painting. However, Dartmoor was his favourite subject, and he enjoyed it for itself, not just as something to paint. Photographs exist showing him at work on the moor, with his painting apparatus round him, and looking rather like G K Chesterton.

William Crossing told the story in his *Dartmoor Worker* (1903) of Widgery painting on the moor when:

> *A passer-by who had a slight acquaintance with him stopped to look over his shoulder at his work. He could not recognise the view before him as that which the artist was painting. In the foreground instead of a marsh there appeared a rocky stream. 'Mr Widgery,' said the visitor mildly, 'there is no river at the foot of that hill.' 'Isn't there?' returned the artist, without looking up, 'well there ought to be.'*

Official photograph of F J Widgery in his mayoral robes.
COURTESY OF RAMM

One wonders if the passer-by was Crossing himself. Crossing writes in his *Dartmoor Worker* that William Widgery was a 'pioneer of Dartmoor painting'.

Four very large oil paintings by William Widgery hang on the wall of the Cavendish function room in the Thistle (formerly the Rougemont) Hotel, Queen Street, Exeter. These are Dartmoor border scenes with trees and running water, and two are of Lydford Gorge. One is painted below the road bridge looking up, a truly dramatic aspect. As well as the four large paintings, there are two by the same artist of coastal scenes on the same wall. This could with advantage be renamed the 'Widgery Room'.

One of Widgery's patrons was Kent Kingdon, a Unitarian wood craftsman who built the somewhat eccentric Taddyforde House beside New North Road in Exeter in the late nineteenth century. He bought a number of Widgery's paintings, and when he died in 1892 they were bequeathed to the Royal Albert Memorial Museum.

F J Widgery had of course many advantages over his father. Whereas William had no art training, F J went through the whole process. His education began at Exeter Cathedral School, then he went to the Exeter School of Art. From here he progressed to the South Kensington Art Schools, then the Academy in Antwerp. Lastly, he came back to England to study under Hubert von Herkomer at a new art school at Bushey, Hertfordshire.

F J WIDGERY 'Belstone Moors, Dartmoor'. Watercolour 59 x 90cms (above left).

COURTESY J COLLINS & SON

'Fur Tor, Dartmoor'. Watercolour 26.5 x 77cms (above right).

COURTESY J COLLINS & SON

'The Clapper Bridge, Teign Head, Dartmoor'. Watercolour 48.5 x 98cms. Inscribed on original label on reverse 'Old Teign Bridge, Dartmoor, by F J Widgery, bought at Exeter in 1898'. Exhibited at Elands' Art Gallery, Exeter, titled 'Pastures, Teignhead Bridge' by F J Widgery (left).

COURTESY J COLLINS & SON

F J WIDGERY 'Rock pillar at Merivale'. Watercolour 25 x 35cms. One of the pictures reproduced in monochrome in Rowe's Perambulation of Dartmoor, *third edition 1896.*

COURTESY OF RAMM

After such a thorough art education it is perhaps surprising he returned to the provinces, but for whatever reason he came back to Exeter and threw himself into local activities which he carried on alongside his painting. He was soon involved in Freemasonry, the Exeter Rotary Club, and saw service in the 1st Devon and Somerset Royal Engineer Volunteers, rising to Captain. On the civic side, he became a city councillor (he was Mayor in 1903–1904), a Freeman, an Alderman, a Justice of the Peace, and served as a governor of various local boards.

As an artist he followed where his father had tilled the soil. He took over William's studio opposite the museum, and was able to work from a secure financial base. Like his father, F J had a house at Lydford which he used as a second home. It is on the corner of the turning to the village from the A386, opposite the Dartmoor Inn.

Dartmoor enthusiasts know his work best for the 22 watercolours he was commissioned to paint for the 1896 revised edition, the third edition, of Samuel Rowe's *A Perambulation of... Dartmoor...* Unfortunately they had to be reproduced in monochrome, but the originals, fresh and summery in the kind of colours one expects in moorland scenes, are in the Royal Albert Memorial Museum and all appear in colour in the handsome book *A Vision of Dartmoor: Paintings by F J Widgery 1861–1942* with a lengthy introduction by Jane Baker (Gollancz 1988). This book commission for Widgery led to four others between 1902 and 1920, though none were specifically devoted to Dartmoor.

F J WIDGERY 'Glorious Devon'. This poster was executed for the GWR in 1925 and superficially looks like Tavy Cleave, but it is more likely to be of an imaginary location.

COURTESY OF SCIENCE & SOCIETY PICTURE LIBRARY

At their best, F J's paintings have an Elgarian *nobilmente* about them which is entirely appropriate given the period in which they were produced. His art was one expression of the golden age of Dartmoor, the years from about 1885 to the beginning of the First World War. This era saw the publication of the first novels of Eden Phillpotts and those of John Trevena; Baring-Gould's literary output was in full flow, serious archaeological enquiry had begun, and William Crossing was active both in the local press and as an author of (mostly) non-fiction books about the moor. This theme will be returned to later in the book.

Apart from his paintings, F J Widgery was remembered, until recently, wherever Exeter-registered cars were seen. He was mayor of Exeter when car licencing was introduced, and his initials were chosen to identify the city's car number plates. He also had an Exeter suburban road named after him, near Polsloe Bridge.

Of all the Dartmoor artists it is the Widgerys, father and son, who are the best known, and a sample perusal of 50 recent West Country auction catalogues has found as many Widgerys as all the rest of the Dartmoor artists put together. The firm of Tavistock Framing Co. is at present retailing card reproductions of F J Widgery paintings at £1.99 each, as well as limited edition prints, indicating their continued popularity.

In many ways the two painters called Charles E Brittan, father and son, have a similar story to the Widgerys, and their dates run in parallel though one is bound to say that the Brittans never achieved the same local fame.

'The Tavy, near Tavy Cleave, Dartmoor'. Watercolour 35 x 25cms.

COURTESY J COLLINS & SON

Charles E Brittan senior (1837–88) was a professional painter who is remembered more for his pictures of animals, though he did paint Dartmoor as well.

Portrait of Charles E Brittan junior. Undated. Painted by 'Wills'.

PRIVATE COLLECTION

His son **Charles E Brittan junior (1870–1949)** began by painting animals, taught by his father, but progressed to the moorland landscape with any pastured stock being subordinated to the wider scene. Human figures are rare. Brittan senior signed his work C E Brittan or used the monogram CEB. His son signed himself Charles E Brittan. Brittan junior's style matured during his lifetime to become more impressionistic, less melodramatic. He painted in both watercolours and oils, but is best known as a watercolourist. Latterly he favoured the lichen-covered rock or boulder in the foreground.

Examples of both artists' work are held at Plymouth Art Gallery. Brittan junior also painted in Scotland, Cornwall and on Exmoor, and Queen Mary bought a number of his Scottish works when they were on sale at Ackermann's Gallery in Bond Street. He also exhibited at the St James's Galleries.

CHARLES E BRITTAN junior 'Looking down the Meavy Valley'. Oil.

PRIVATE COLLECTION

Like F J Widgery, Brittan junior was commissioned to illustrate books. He provided the cover drawings for the Reverend Hugh Breton's series of *Beautiful Dartmoor* guidebooks. Breton was vicar of Sheepstor at the time. He also did three pictures for the Reverend Sabine Baring-Gould's 1912 book *Sheepstor*, which was produced in aid of the Sheepstor Screen Restoration Fund. In 1911 he illustrated an edition of the Exmoor romantic adventure *Lorna Doone*, and in 1925 provided 12 paintings for Alfred Vowles's *The Lorna Doone Country*.

Brittan lived at Burrator House and is buried in Sheepstor churchyard, though towards the end of his life he lived in Tavistock. William Crossing was moved by Brittan's paintings. He wrote in 1903 in the newspaper article, subsequently published in his *Dartmoor Worker*:

No-one who is not a stranger to it [Dartmoor] can look upon the pictures of Mr Charles E Brittan without being conscious that they breathe its spirit. They are distinguished by a charm of colour, while his effects of light and shade on cloud are wonderful.

An obituary tribute in the *Western Morning News* (1949) included the following:

Brittan was a painter in a class by himself. His works showed a knowledge of Dartmoor flowers and ferns, granite and atmosphere, that could be attained by years of intimate study of the moor, his delineation of which has never been excelled.

His were not the overdone purple hues, but the delicate, subdued, and softer tints that held one's admiration by their charm, beauty and fidelity. He has made Dartmoor live, and Devon has lost a great artist.'

After the Widgerys, it is probably the paintings of the Morrish family which appear most frequently on the market. Of these, **William Snell Morrish (1844–1917)** was the most prolific, and is certainly the best known.

He was born in Chagford, the son of another **William Morrish (1812–67)**, who had married Ann Snell in 1841. The father is listed in the 1851 Census as being a 'draper, grocer, artist and portrait painter', but little else is known of him. To return to W S Morrish.

He trained at the Exeter School of Art and in London, and Pycroft (*Art in Devonshire* 1883) writes of him:

...his chief source of instruction was the work and conversation of the artists who in summer visited his picturesque neighbourhood. He paints with a bold, firm touch in the open air; his work is characterised by perfect fidelity and truthfulness, and he is an admirable delineator of Dartmoor scenery.

W S MORRISH 'A Moorland Stream' 1879. Watercolour 26 x 74cms.

COURTESY J COLLINS & SON

W S MORRISH 'A Woodland Stream'. Watercolour 51 x 53cms

COURTESY J COLLINS & SON

'A group of Chagford anglers'. W S Morrish is sitting at the front, on the right.

COURTESY OF SIMON HILL AND FAMILY

This confirms that Chagford was a popular haunt of artists in the 1860s and 1870s. He was also friendly with other well-known artists of the time – Frederick Barnard, John Skinner Prout and John H Mole.

As a young man he had painted in Switzerland and in northern Italy, but settled back in Chagford, and established himself in his studio overlooking the Square above the shop which is now (2002) Youd's newsagents. It was probably here that he was visited by a journalist in the late 1860s, who wrote up his encounter in *Devonshire Sketches: Dartmoor and its Borders*. The author called himself Tickler, but was really E Tozer. The chapters were originally printed as articles in the *Devon Weekly Times*.

> *I was invited to visit the studio of a native painter, Mr Morrish. I found the artist a young man of simple and unaffected manners, excellent qualities which usually appear in persons of genuine merit. His pictures, representing the lovely scenery of the neighbourhood, are very promising evidences of 'grit' as Brother Jonathon would say. Wishing the worthy young man a bright and prosperous future, I passed on with my companions...*

Morrish became an institution in Chagford. He entered fully into the life of the town, and being fond of music, assisted the Chagford Band, the orchestral society and concert parties in every way. He exhibited regularly at Elands' Gallery in Exeter and at the Royal Academy. He favoured the upper North Teign River, and liked to take his easel out on to the moor to enable him to paint direct from nature. He is known to have given pictures to fellow Chagfordians to settle debts. He died at Blandford House, Chagford, in 1917 at the age of 73.

His eldest surviving son was **Bertram Morrish (1878–?)**, who has been known to be referred to as Bernard, but this is incorrect. Like his father, he was a prolific painter, and his style is similar. He eventually married and moved to London. He had a son and daughter. Bertram is mentioned in *Hidden Talents*.

The last of the Morrish painting clan, though any true relationship is unknown, was **Sydney** (sometimes **Sidney**) **S Morrish (1836–?)**. There is in the Devon & Exeter Institution an annotated copy of *Art In Devonshire* (Pycroft 1883) and someone – possibly Pycroft himself – has added some biographical lines about Sydney S Morrish:

> *Of Clare House, Torquay. An excellent painter of cottage interiors and landscapes in oil. Also painted portraits. Born Exeter 1836. Studied at the Art School of Mr Cary, Bloomsbury Square, and at the Royal Academy. His landscapes have been exhibited at the Royal Academy and are of great merit. Mr Morrish took up residence in Torquay in 1871, and was appointed Master of the School of Art in 1877, which he held for ten years. He loves to paint his native county, especially the banks of the Dart and Teign.*

Two oil paintings by Sydney S Morrish titled 'Domestic Peace' and 'Dartmoor' are listed in the *Catalogue of Paintings on Display at Torre Abbey, Torquay* (L Retallick, reprinted in 1986).

William Williams (1808–95) is a painter who has grown in stature in recent years. Although he was born in Penryn, Cornwall, he moved to Devon early in life, and, to save confusion with the many other artists called Williams, signed his work 'William Williams (of) Plymouth'. He was unconnected with the other Williams family. He had an address in Bath, which may have simply been an accommodation address, but later moved from Plymouth to Torquay and Topsham.

There were 18 William Williams's paintings exhibited at *The Devonshire Scene* exhibition of 1973 of which six were undoubtedly of Dartmoor, and the 18 covered a forty-five year span from 1845 to 1890. The 1986 catalogue of paintings at Torre Abbey lists four by William Williams, one of which is definitely of Dartmoor. Phillips's catalogue for their June 1998 sale shows an early William Williams watercolour of 1830 titled 'Figures, cattle and sheep in an extensive landscape with Dartmoor in the distance'. Sixty-two years later he painted an oil 'Early morning on the river Dart, Holne, Devon', and this picture was illustrated in J Collins & Son's catalogue for May 1997. He had a lengthy active life.

Williams preferred to paint in oil, if the number of his oil paintings is anything to go by, and when cleaned they look as fresh as if they were executed last week. One senses with this painter that the professional artist is becoming more adventurous and pushing up on to the moor, but there were others doing this at the same time. He died in Topsham.

WILLIAM WILLIAMS 'On the Dart', a pair. Oil on mahogany panel and oil on board, both 38 x 24cms.
COURTESY J COLLINS & SON

His son was christened **Roscoe Sheddon Goodrich Williams (1852–c.1922)**, and was born in Topsham. He preferred to be known as S G W Roscoe, and as such appears in Mallalieu's *The Dictionary of British Watercolour Artists up to 1920*. He trained with his father and at the Exeter and West London Schools of Art, and exhibited from 1874 to 1888 with views of Devon, Yorkshire, Surrey, North Wales, and Scotland. He was an enthusiastic sailor.

Another father-and-son pairing of artists with Dartmoor connections was **Daniel Sherrin RBA (1868–1940)** and **Reginald Daniel Sherrin (1891–1971)**. The father spent most of his life in south-east England where he was known for his marine landscapes. His own father, John Sherrin RI (1819–96), was also an artist but did not paint on Dartmoor. Daniel Sherrin's Dartmoor work is scarce as he seems only to have visited the moor when he came to Devon to see his son who had moved there. His 'Dartmoor Landscape with Distant Tor' was sold at Phillips's Powderham Castle sale of 29 June 1999.

R D Sherrin's paintings are frequently seen, and he also labelled his pictures with the pseudonym 'J Whiteley' or 'D A Neil'. The latter is a reshaping of his second Christian name. His style is similar to that of F J Widgery.

There is often confusion between **George Henry Jenkins (1843–1914)** and his son **George Henry Jenkins (1866–1937)**, particularly as they both lived in Plymouth. William Crossing remarks in his *Dartmoor Worker* that Jenkins senior's '… works show how closely he has studied Dartmoor'. The father also has an entry in *Hidden Talents*. Jenkins junior's paintings appear fairly regularly at auction. Some of his pictures were used by Raphael Tuck for sale as postcards.

G H JENKINS junior 'On the Lyd, near Okehampton' (below left) and 'Taw Marsh'. Two of a series of postcards published by Raphael Tuck.

AUTHOR'S COLLECTION

Dartmoor becomes popular with artists

Mention has been made in an earlier chapter of the publication in 1848 of Samuel Rowe's *A Perambulation of the Antient and Royal Forest of Dartmoor* for which the illustrator was Charles F Williams. This sent out a signal that there was an expanse of high ground called Dartmoor, which was different from the rest of Devon, possessed antiquities without number, and was worth the trouble of exploration.

Publication coincided with the arrival of the railway in the county, the development of photography and the opening of the convict prison at Princetown in 1850. The later chapters of *Dartmoor: A New Study* chronicle the changes at this time, so it is on the back of these developments, which meant that Dartmoor was entering modern times, that subsequent artistic and literary endeavour must be seen.

One of the first truly local artists to earn a living from the moor was **Frederick Foot (1831–1908)**. He came from an Ashburton family, and is buried in the cemetery there – almost at the far end of the long churchyard – beneath a headstone bearing an artist's palette and easel. The inscription reads:

In
Loving Memory of
Frederick Foot
Artist
Youngest son of
Peter Foot
Who died at Lustleigh
Feb 4th 1908
Aged 77

Frederick Foot's gravestone in Ashburton churchyard bearing palette and easel.

PHOTOGRAPH BY KEN NOTT

A drawing by Foot of Silverbrook Mine, Ilsington, can be found on page 36 of Helen Harris's book *The Industrial Archaeology of Dartmoor*, and is one of very few images of work and labour which artists bothered to paint. Two pencil drawings by Foot of the Old Market House, Ashburton, illustrate J S Amery's Presidential Address to the Devonshire Association of 1924 (Volume 56). His work comes on the market from time to time and is quickly snapped up. It often depicts the River Dart or elsewhere on the south-eastern moor.

An informative two-page illustrated article by the late Dave Brewer, 'Frederick Foot and Dartmoor', was published in the *Dartmoor Magazine* no 41 (winter 1995), and lists many of his works. A number of his

FREDERICK FOOT 'On the Dart' 1856. Oil 68 x 90cms. This impressive painting of Lovers' Leap by the 25-year-old artist was on sale for £2695 on the stand of the Mill Gallery at Westpoint, near Exeter, in November 2001.

COURTESY MILL GALLERY

sketches are kept in Torquay Museum. Of all Dartmoor artists he was the one who most frequently drew mines and mills.

A London-based artist and illustrator James Thorpe, who retired to Dean Prior, wrote a late autobiography called *Happy Days: Recollections of an Unrepentant Victorian* (1933), in which he states that Frederick Foot 'had a considerable local reputation as a landscape painter'. He added that Frederick's brother Edward, wrote poetry of the 'sublimely and unconsciously ridiculous' kind. One feels that a study of Frederick Foot and his work would be a rewarding task for a researcher.

John Henry Mole RI (1814–86) is known to have painted in the Chagford area. He liked to include children in his compositions, and his picture 'Watermill near Chagford, Devon, with Children making Daisy-chains' is illustrated in H L Mallalieu's *The Dictionary of British Watercolour Artists up to 1920, Volume 2, The Plates*.

It is always difficult for a son to follow in the footsteps of a famous father, and when he is given the same name it is doubly hard. But **David Cox junior ARWS (1809–55)** although not as gifted as his parent made his mark in his own way. In an article about Cox junior in *The Old Water-Colour Society's Club Sixtieth Annual Volume* (1985) Ian Cooke writes of him as 'a fine artist of middle rank'. Cox made two visits to Devon, in 1865 and 1877, and on the second trip he executed a watercolour of Okehampton viewed from the hill to the south which illustrates Cooke's article. In letters Cox described the Devon scenery as 'painterly'.

Arthur Henry Enoch RHA RSA RI (fl 1869–1912) was admired by William Crossing for 'his evening scenes', and I have seen one of his watercolours captioned 'The Evening Glow, Postbridge, Dartmoor' which portrays this preference. His technique was similar to that of F J Widgery, without having the polish, and this is reflected in the present-day auction prices which tend to be in three figures. Mallalieu gives him ten lines and states that after he became fully professional in 1890 and moved to Devon from the Midlands he became known as 'the artist of the Dart'. He also painted Totnes and the lower reaches of the Dart, and lived at Dartmouth, Torquay and Newton Abbot.

The only reason the name of **Arthur James Stark (1831–1902)** appears here is on the strength of his lively oil 'Dartmoor Drift' which depicts the annual round-up, known as the drift, of Dartmoor ponies. This painting was presented to the Royal Albert Memorial Museum in 1945 by the artist's son, Mr J A Stark, and is on sale as a postcard. The painter's connection with the moor is not known, but another painting by Stark titled 'Dartmoor Ponies' is held at the Castle Museum, Norwich. The artist's father James Stark (1794–1859) was a leader of the Norwich School. Arthur Stark trained at the Royal Academy Schools, exhibited at the Royal Academy 36 times, and 'Dartmoor Drift' was one of these.

ARTHUR J STARK 'Dartmoor Drift'. Oil on canvas 104 x 183cms. A drift on Dartmoor is an animal roundup.

COURTESY OF RAMM

William Crossing had a high opinion of **Arthur Bevan Collier (fl 1850–1900)**. He wrote in his article 'The Artist' in the *Dartmoor Worker*:

> *Probably none of our Dartmoor artists knows the moor better than Mr A B Collier, who was painting it more than half a century ago, and still continues to do so. And it is certain that no artist is more true to his original. In his pictures the features of the moor are never exaggerated; one does not find the tors made to look like the Grampians.*

He is first listed as living at 74 Newman Street, London in 1855, but later moved to Tavistock, Plympton, Sampford Spiney, Launceston and finally Callington. He provided some of the illustrations for Sabine Baring-Gould's *A Book of Dartmoor* (1900), and two of his pictures are reproduced in Pauline Hemery's *The Book of Meavy* (1999). During a long active life he exhibited 21 paintings at the Royal Academy.

John William Salter (1825–1891) was, according to a report in the *Western Morning News* of 15 December 1998, born into the farming community of North Tawton, in Mid Devon. He left home in the 1840s to study engraving in London, and while there also worked for *The Illustrated London News*. He established a studio in Torquay in 1850 as a 'Professor of Drawing' though he also taught oil and water-colour painting, and became known as 'Salter of Torquay'.

JOHN SALTER 'Buckland-in-the-Moor' 1888. Watercolour 24 x 38cms. Available as a postcard from Torquay Museum (opposite).
COURTESY TORQUAY MUSEUM

JOHN SALTER 'On the Wallabrook, Gidleigh' 1881. Watercolour (right).
COURTESY TORQUAY MUSEUM

Mallalieu writes that 'it is probable that he should be identified with' another Salter having the same Christian names who was an FGS, and who worked on the Geological Survey of the UK and Canada from the 1840s to the 1860s.

Torre Abbey has only two paintings by him, but Torquay Museum has a greater number, including several Dartmoor scenes. A very attractive watercolour of the thatched cottages at Buckland-in-the-Moor was used by Devon Books for the dust-jacket of *The Old Devon Farmhouse* by Peter Brears (1998). He is also known to have painted along the south coast of England and in Yorkshire, Wales, Northumberland, Ireland and Italy.

Little is known of **John Barrett (fl 1875–1900)** except that he was based in Plymouth and usually painted in watercolour, though oils are known. His work is represented in Plymouth Art Gallery, and comes up at auction quite regularly when it is seen to show Dartmoor scenery in all its splendour. A layer of mist in the middle distance is one of his characteristics, and his paintings found favour with William Crossing. A delightful picture, 'Girls gathering daisies at Roborough', is known.

Painting Dartmoor at the same time was **Arthur Suker (fl 1882–1902)** who came from a family of artists, though they tried not to get in each other's way. His brother changed his name to Newcombe to make his own career, and his first cousin was Walter Crane RWS, who had several relatives who were active painters though not of Dartmoor. Arthur Suker was born in Cheshire in 1857 and trained at the Birkenhead School of Art, later painting in Wales, the Lake District, the Channel Islands and the Isle of Man. He used oil and watercolour and I have seen examples of his work set near Belstone, Dartmeet and Brimpts. He favoured views of fast-flowing rivers.

In 1970 the author wrote in *Dartmoor: A New Study*:

> *In retrospect one realises that the thirty or so years from about 1885 to the start of the First World War were the golden years for Dartmoor.*

There is no need to repeat the reasons I set out then but the reader will have gathered that the art scene was burgeoning like so many other aspects of Dartmoor life. A contributory factor was the success of R D Blackmore's romantic adventure story *Lorna Doone*, set on Exmoor and published in 1869. This book helped the growing appreciation of high moorland scenery in what is called the Heroic period.

In 1888 J Fortescue was writing in *The Magazine of Art* as follows:

> *The tourist reads Lorna Doone, buys a guidebook and hies him to the Doones's combe – if it be a fine day. He turns his back on the Badgworthy gorge and all its loveliness, and feasts his romantic vision on the grass-grown foundations of what was very likely a pig's house. It is enough for him. These ruins are, as he is told, the Doones's houses; and Nature has no charms for him unless consecrated by the holy ink of the novelist.*

There seem to have been few associational attractions to draw artists to Dartmoor. Eden Phillpotts never pulled painters to the moor as Hardy did to Dorset, Blackmore to Exmoor, or Kingsley to Clovelly. Perhaps the all-action illustrations of **Sidney Paget (1860–1908)** which enlivened *The Hound of the Baskervilles* in *The Strand Magazine* serialisation had an effect. All the activity seemed to take place after dark, and a gloomy twilight world is sometimes portrayed in early twentieth century Dartmoor paintings. A set of six postcards painted by Andrew Beer (see pages 64 and 81), all showing a full moon, and clearly meant to be night-time views, were on sale at this time.

SIDNEY PAGET 'I saw the figure of a man upon the tor' (above). *'There he sat upon a stone'* (left). *Two of Sidney Paget's illustrations for the* The Strand Magazine *in which 'The Hound of the Baskervilles' was serialised, starting in August 1901. The reader will decide for himself or herself whether Paget ever visited Dartmoor.*

AUTHOR'S COLLECTION

ANDREW BEER 'Hay Tor' (above left). *'Leather Tor and Bridge'* (right). *Two postcards from a set of six.*
AUTHOR'S COLLECTION

Incidentally, *The Hound of the Baskervilles* film portrayal of Dartmoor, as represented by the Basil Rathbone version (he made 14 films as Sherlock Holmes), has had a lasting effect on the public's perception of Dartmoor: stage mist, rectangular rocks, the obligatory escaped prisoner, and the bottomless bog, are all clichés of Dartmoor imagery.

The first photographer to make a significant impact on Dartmoor was **Robert Burnard FSA JP (1848–1920)**. Burnard was a successful Plymouth businessman who developed a deep interest in Dartmoor. From 1887 he began a photographic record of the moor which resulted in a collection of about 700 pictures being built up. Between 1890 and 1894 he published, at his own expense, the four volumes of *Dartmoor Pictorial Records*. Each contained between 15 and 19 of his photographs with the addition of descriptive text, maps, plans and woodcuts. Only 150 copies of Volume 1 were printed and 200 of each of the remaining three volumes. His work has a permanent value as he chose subjects which subsequently dated.

In 1972 the Royal Albert Memorial Museum in Exeter arranged an exhibition of his photographs, many of them from the albums then in the possession of Burnard's grand-daughter, Lady Sayer. In 1986 Devon Books republished the four volumes of *Dartmoor Pictorial Records* in a facsimile edition limited to 1000 copies. This brought his art to the notice of a new generation of Dartmoor enthusiasts. His photographic legacy was further strengthened in 2000 when Devon Books in association with the Dartmoor Trust published *Dartmoor Century: Photography on Dartmoor Across a Hundred Years*, with many of Burnard's photographs reproduced beside contemporary views. In his introduction to this book, Simon Butler has written:

> *Though photography and art have remained uneasy bedfellows, the exceptional photograph (whether through its 'artistic' content, or because it captures a dramatic moment in time) has always been prized. At what moment a photograph becomes important simply because of its historic value is less clear.*

Robert Burnard on the banks of the Dart below Huccaby (opposite).

The chair in Dunnabridge Pound, c.1892 (left). *Brownberry, the thatched farmhouse across the road, has disappeared since the photograph was taken.*

Ponsworthy water splash c.1892 (below left).

THOMAS A FALCON Title page for Pictorial Dartmoor *1902, 21.5 x 28cms* (top). *The cover is of stout grey paper stitched to the 54 photographs* (below).
AUTHOR'S COLLECTION

The publication of *Dartmoor Illustrated* by **Thomas Adolphus Falcon RBA MA (1872–1944)** in 1900 brought the work of this young artist before the public. He was a landscape painter, born in Yorkshire, who lived in Braunton, North Devon, from 1901 until his death. He exhibited two pictures at the Royal Academy and 138 as a member of the Royal Society of British Artists. He designed the attractive Arts & Crafts cover and title page for his 1902 book *Pictorial Dartmoor* which must have raised a few eyebrows one hundred years ago.

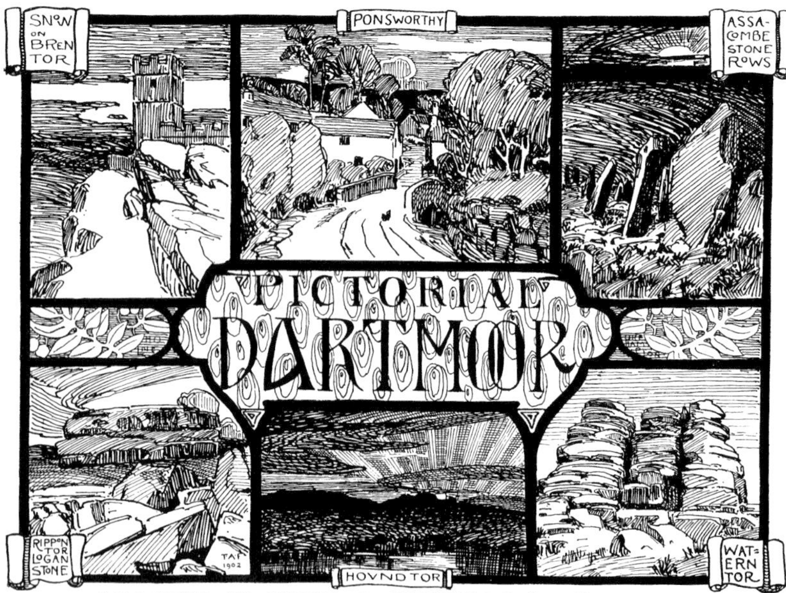

'Meldon Viaduct'. It is possible that this picture, date unknown, was prepared for use by the London & South Western Railway as a poster (right).
PRIVATE COLLECTION

Dartmoor Illustrated was commissioned by the publisher as companion or supplement to the Brooking Rowe 1896 revised edition of Samuel Rowe's *Perambulation of Dartmoor*, and indeed they have matching covers. There were no photographs in this edition, only F J Widgery's 22 watercolours reproduced in monochrome. It has to be said that Falcon's photographs are not special, but his commentaries have a personal touch. For instance, in describing Spinster's Rock he writes:

> *...the only Devonian standing cromlech reigns in a potato field, or haply over turnips and mangolds. Its dignity somehow survives the contest with those strenuous vegetables; but many must needs think congruity more important than locality, and regret the domesticity of its setting.*

The West Country Studies Library has a collection of his pen and ink drawings and some watercolours. Two of these wash drawings appear on the dust-jacket of the 1987 Devon Books facsimile edition of *The Ancient Stone Crosses of Dartmoor and its Borderland* by William Crossing (1902). Nine of his small wash drawings of crosses appear in *Dartmoor Stone Crosses* by Bill Harrison (Halsgrove 2001).

Perhaps the supreme Dartmoor image-maker for the greater part of the twentieth century was the Dawlish firm of **Chapman & Son**, photographers and retailers of black and white postcards. These are invariably identified by the back-handed captions with negative numbers. Many of the photographs were taken by a second-generation family member, **W S Chapman (1859–1918)**, who penetrated to nearly all the towns, villages and even hamlets in South Devon. Later he widened his range, extending outwards to Cornwall and Surrey. The Second World War almost closed the firm but it limped on until 1967. Fortunately the historic glass-plate negatives were passed to the Devon Record Office. The full story is told in a fascinating little book *Chapman's Devon in Camera* by Raymond Worden (Quotes, Buckingham 1987).

CHAPMAN & SON 'Badger's Holt cafe, Dartmeet' (below left) and 'The Fireplace, Becky Falls, Manaton'. Two typical postcards produced by this Dawlish firm.

AUTHOR'S COLLECTION

The paintings of **Tom Rowden (1842–1926)** are often seen at sales of Dartmoor pictures and are almost invariably of animals, whether ponies, cattle or sheep, in a moorland scene, perhaps with a mist-shrouded tor in the background and a stream flowing past. He seems to have cornered the market in Dartmoor livestock, a trait remarked upon by William Crossing in 1903. He was self-taught and lived in Exeter from about 1890. As well as Dartmoor he painted the Scottish Highlands and the Cornish coast.

Active at the same time was **Harold Lawes (fl 1885–1920)**, whose only known address is at Primrose Hill, London, but who must have had a Devon base from time to time. The pictures I have seen are of the Chagford and River Teign area, and are competently painted. A good Lawes painting will change hands for a four-figure sum.

The Dartmoor paintings of **William John Caparne FRHS (1855–1940)** have only become known and collectable during the last few years but his story is a strange one and worth the telling.

He was born in Nottingham and in due course became assistant drawing master at Oundle School. He had always been interested in horticulture, and in the 1870s began to paint every variety of iris and daffodil. He travelled around England, Wales, Ireland and the Channel Islands, and took parties of boys from Oundle to the Lake District.

His wife died in 1894, and this event, coupled with school reorganisation, seems to have unsettled him. At all events he left the area and his dearly loved garden and moved to a rented cottage near Ashburton in 1896. He also added an 'e' to his name. He now began to paint right across Dartmoor, and nearly 200 watercolours are known, ranging from Holne Chase to Tavy Cleave, and from Belstone to Goodameavy. These are listed and numbered in a well-illustrated 102-page monograph about Caparne, written by his present-day champion the Tavistock art dealer and auctioneer Robin A. Fenner, *A Genius Undeclared* published by Robin Fenner in 1994.

In 1897 Caparne settled in Guernsey, although he travelled abroad to many European destinations and on one trip met Claude Monet. He twice returned to Dartmoor, in 1901 and 1904. He and his unmarried daughter Winifred established themselves in St Martin's parish, on the cliffs above Bon Port, and here Caparne used an old single-decker Guernsey tramcar as his studio. (The author, then a boy of eight or nine and living in Guernsey, remembers seeing this strange cliff-top aberration when out for family cliff-top walks in the immediate pre-war years.) But Caparne made little money from his pictures. His main source of income, and that of his daughter, was derived from his Iris Plant & Bulb Company.

William J Caparne painting outside his tramcar studio on the Guernsey cliffs in the 1930s.

COURTESY OF ROBIN A FENNER

Caparne's eyesight deteriorated during the last four years of his life, and from the summer of 1938 he was totally blind. He died on 31 January 1940 and five months later the German forces occupied the island. Miss Winifred Caparne had no choice but to remain on the island. She had no regular income but managed to sell off some of her father's pictures to German officers, and cultivated vegetables in the now-derelict flower plots. At the end of the war she sold up and moved to Exmouth with 8000 paintings and not much else. When she died in 1972 she bequeathed the remaining 7800 pictures to the Dean and Chapter of Exeter Cathedral. There then followed an unhappy episode. Advice was questionable and disposal erratic, and many pictures were damaged by damp. Others were incinerated but eventually those that survived found their way via reputable dealers to purchasers who cared for them and W J Caparne's pictures are at last bringing pleasure to art lovers.

As has been said, there was no Dartmoor School as such, but the influence of the Widgerys, father and son, had an effect on other painters, and **H Sinclair Jackson (fl 1887–96)** was one of these. He was a friend of F J Widgery and it is known they visited Dartmoor on painting exhibitions. He lived in South Avenue, Exeter. He exhibited at Elands, Art Gallery in Exeter, and usually painted in watercolour, though oils are not unknown. An oil titled 'Near the Gate on the Moor, Dartmoor' was sold by J Collins & Son in 1996. It shows an expanse of moor, perhaps with a hazy Steeperton Tor in the background and a slow-flowing river in the foreground passing through a reed-grown marsh.

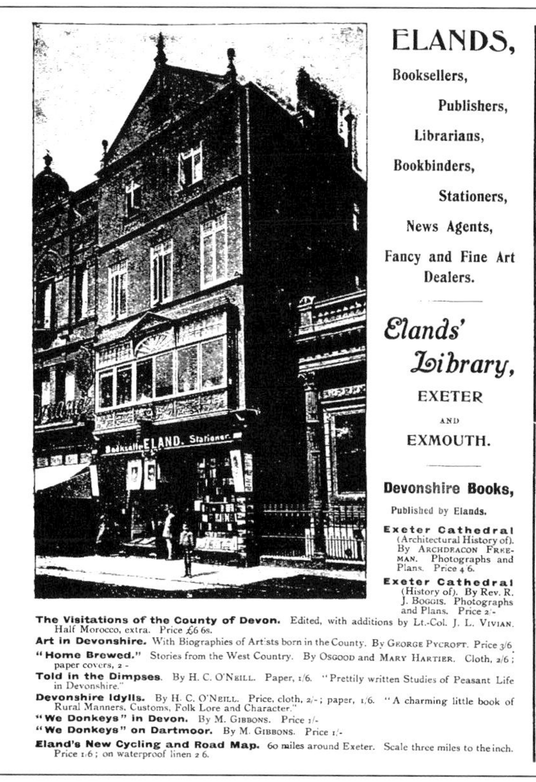

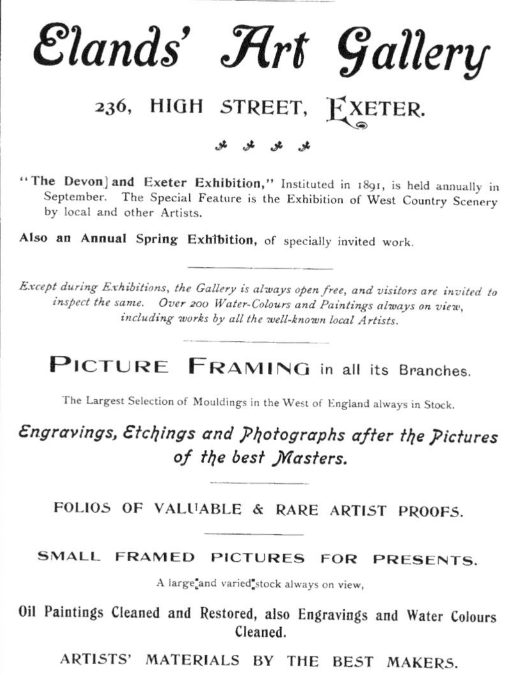

ELANDS' ART GALLERY (exterior) and advertisement page. Elands was an important retail outlet for Devon artists. Copied from the advertisement section at back of Pictorial Dartmoor *by T A Falcon 1902. Note that Pycroft's* Art in Devonshire *is still for sale for 3s 6d (17½p) nineteen years after first being published by Elands. The squat classical building to the right of Elands was the Commercial Union, with a statue of King Alfred over the door. These buildings were between the present Lloyds TSB and Gandy Street, and were destroyed in 1942.*

AUTHOR'S COLLECTION

ELANDS' ART GALLERY (interior). Photograph taken during an exhibition. Copied from small pocket-sized red-covered guide, The Borough Pocket Guide, Exeter no 2 *United Devon Association 1909.*

AUTHOR'S COLLECTION

George Shaw (1843–1915) seems to have painted only in oil. He was born in Derby but after a spell in Worcester and then the USA, lived in Exeter, painted in the vicinity – particularly on Dartmoor – and exhibited locally and at least once at the Royal Academy. He also lived at Exmouth and Torquay, and died at Rewe just outside Exeter. Eight of his paintings were sold by Phillips at their Powderham Castle sale in June 2000, and a large, slightly damaged painting by Shaw of 'Cranmere Pool' was sold by Greenslade Taylor Hunt of Taunton for £190 in November 2000. He is given 22 lines in *Hidden Talents*.

John Baragwanath King (1864–1939) was born near Penzance, and initially trained as an engineer, before becoming a professional painter in oils and watercolours of landscape and coastal scenes. His studio was in Connaught Avenue, Plymouth, and from here he was able to paint both Dartmoor and Cornwall views. He exhibited in London, Paris and other Continental centres, and his work was purchased by King Edward VII and

Queen Alexandra. He later moved to St Austell. William Crossing wrote in 1903, 'Who that has seen Baragwanath King's border scenes will not admit their fidelity, or that of his pictures of the moor when it wears its summer garb of purple?' King's pictures turn up at auction fairly regularly, and as Crossing suggested, they are often of the Dartmoor fringes. A painting of Lydford Gorge is at Lanhydrock House and I have seen several of his works showing the River Tavy. He was a proficient artist who painted both large and small pictures.

William Henry Dyer (fl c.1890–1930) has a lengthy reference in *Hidden Talents*. He lived at Babbacombe, Torquay, but travelled extensively in Switzerland, Italy, Egypt and India. Beside his water-colours and oils, he illustrated postcards published by J Salmon. The same publisher produced a scarce book (undated) of 15 images called *Dartmoor: From Original Water Colour Paintings*. A collection of 15 Dyer watercolours, some of Scotland and the Lake District, was sold at Phillips sale Exeter in June 1999. The estimated selling price in all cases was less than £100.

Like Frederick Foot, **Sidney Endacott (1873–1918)** was born in Ashburton, the fifth of seven sons. He was educated at Ashburton Grammar School then got a scholarship to Blundell's School. He trained as a woodcarver before following two of his brothers to Kansas. His major commission here was to decorate a mansion built by a retired Civil War officer, General J N Roberts, by using different woods for the various rooms. 'The Castle', as it came to be known, is now on the National Register of Historic Places.

But Sidney saw little future in Kansas which he regarded as a frontier area, so he returned to Devon and worked for J Wippell & Company of Exeter, the church furnishers. He then became a freelance, lectured at Exeter Art College, and produced paintings of the Devon landscape. This developed into the production of several series of postcards, mostly published by Worths of Exeter, but it is not for his Dartmoor images that he is known, though occasional moorland views come to light.

Sidney married **Lillie (Lily) Haydon (1885–1952)** in 1903 and taught her to paint, so when he died a few days before the end of the First World War she carried on producing postcards. She died in 1952 and was buried at the Higher Cemetery, Exeter, with Sidney, in a grave marked, like that of Frederick Foot, by a gravestone bearing an artist's easel and palette. Husband and wife are given considerable space in *Hidden Talents*.

Another notable Ashburton artist – a photographer – was **Miss Amy Satterly (1881–1965)**. She was twice married, to Mr Hannaford and Mr White, but seems to have traded under her maiden name. Pete Webb wrote an article about her in the *Dartmoor Magazine* no 50 (spring 1998) illustrated by eight of her pictures. She published postcards, and the one of Widecombe church tower enveloped in scaffolding and dated 1906, is a worthy image. Amy's brother (Jack in the family) emigrated to Canada in 1912, became Professor John Satterly of Toronto University, and was one of the team that first split the atom. His paper 'Memories of Ashburton in late Victorian Days' occupies 31 pages of the *Transactions* of the Devonshire Association for 1952.

The small watercolour by **Herbert Arnould (or Arnold) Oliver RI RP RE RBC (1861–1952)** which was sold by J Collins & Son in October 1994 is the only picture I have seen by this artist. It is a pleasant conventional view of the Walla Brook clapper bridge, looking west with Watern Tor on the skyline and a few cattle in the middle distance. This artist was born in Battle, educated at Sherborne, and studied at the Royal Academy Schools where he won the Creswick Prize in 1883. He painted in oil and watercolour. He was an official war artist and his work is in the Imperial War Museum. He died at Haying Island.

The link of **Augustus John OM (1878–1961)** with Dartmoor is slight, and appears to be limited to a few weeks in the spring and summer of 1905. He had bought a gypsy caravan from a friend, Michel Salaman, which was beside a stream and not far from the Warren House Inn, and here his mistress Dorelia came to give birth to their baby boy, Pyramus. The child's birth was never registered, but John wrote in a letter that he thought it was in the parish of Lydford.

The other components of the *ménage à trois* were not present. John's wife Ida was in Essex, and John himself in Liverpool, but a telegram brought them separately to Dartmoor and they were joined a few days later by Ida's three children, aged three, two and six months, presumably brought down by an adult. Mr and Mrs Hext at the inn had arranged for a doctor and nurse to minister to Dorelia's needs. John made himself useful at the camp by constructing a tent annexe to the caravan in the gypsy fashion, and spent time at the inn with the Hexts. He went off on sketching expeditions and produced several works. In the publication *Augustus John* by Robert Shone (Phaidon 1979) there is a colour reproduction of a 1905 picture 'Ida in the Tent', probably the tent John provided. The picture is noted as being in a Private Collection.

Anthony Greenstreet's article in the *Dartmoor Magazine* no 44 (autumn 1996) titled 'A Dartmoor Birth' is illustrated by a painting of a gypsy encampment on Dartmoor dated the following year, but with something like a Dartmoor tor to one side. It shows two women and two children, and the woman standing between the shafts of the caravan is plainly modelled on Dorelia. Pyramus died when only six from meningitis to his father's great distress. He was cremated at Woking but when John travelled home by train with the ashes he put the urn on the luggage rack, forgetting it when he got off. There is a happy end to the story as the urn was later returned to the grieving parents.

AUGUSTUS JOHN 'Gypsy encampment on Dartmoor' 1906.

PRIVATE COLLECTION. PHOTOGRAPH COURTESY OF COURTAULD INSTITUTE OF ART

Alfred Leyman (1856–1933) was probably born in Exeter, though *Hidden Talents* suggests Honiton. He was briefly a seaman in the Merchant Navy but moved to Honiton around 1888 and became art master at Allhallows School in 1893, staying there until 1933. The school holidays enabled him to wander around the county and paintings of Clovelly, the Teign Estuary, Seaton, Dartmouth and Kingswear are common. Other favourite subjects were Exeter and eastern Dartmoor. The author has seen watercolours of Dunsford from the same viewpoint, but with different matters of detail. Lustleigh was another favourite subject. A former pupil of his at Allhallows School has written:

> *He was a smallish man and a very shy one. I feel now that he had no real teaching ability, and that he would have been happier alone with his easel, and away from rumbustuous boys, painting the countryside he loved so much.*

The reputation of **Philip Guy Stevens FGS (1883–1944)** has only developed since the publication of the Peninsula Press edition of *Crossing's Guide to Dartmoor* in 1990. Before then he was really only known for the black and white sketches which he drew to illustrate the *Guide*, and which were hardly art. But the Peninsula Press reproduced eight of his paintings in this edition, together with a four-page biographical note about Stevens written by his grandson Andrew, so we now know more about him and his work. He painted in oil and watercolour, and to a good standard. Even before the First World War he was exhibiting at Harris's West of England Gallery in Plymouth.

His working life began as a teacher in Topsham, but his father persuaded him to join the Prison Service. He became a clerk at Dartmoor Prison, and it was while here that he was asked by William Crossing to illustrate the book that became the *Guide to Dartmoor*. He married Beatrice, the daughter of Aaron Rowe of the Duchy Hotel in 1909. His first move was to Leeds, then came the war, and a return to Princetown after. Promotion to Swansea followed, and it was while here that he was head-hunted to become governor of Shrewsbury Prison and later Norwich. Such a move from the clerical side of prison administration to that of governor was almost unheard of at the time. He retired early through ill health in 1938, and went to live in Somerton, Somerset, where he died in 1944. He is buried in Princetown.

His son Alan, who after a career in banking, enjoyed retirement in Drewsteignton, possessed a number of his father's paintings, and had stickers printed which he applied to the back of the pictures before giving some of them away. He gave me one in 1978 which bears the wording:

A Somerset Scene
1941
by
Philip Guy Stevens FGS
1883–1944
Illustrator of
Crossing's Guide to Dartmoor

Rubens A J N Southey (1881–1933) is a shadowy figure who is likely to have been born in Wellington, Somerset, though Exeter also has a claim on him, a suggested birthdate being 1875. He lived in South Wales, Plymouth, Barnstaple, Teignmouth and Ashburton. His paintings are usually in watercolour, and are mostly of coastal or moorland scenes. After developing arthritis he painted little towards the end of his life, and died in Newton Abbot.

In contrast, the life and work of **John Shapland (1865–1929)** is well documented. The 1994 autumn watercolour exhibition catalogue of J Collins & Son has a two-page biography of this artist, as well as monochrome images of the 67 pictures which were on sale. Only two or three of these are indisputably of Dartmoor, and there is no way of knowing if this was a fair representation of his moorland work.

Shapland was born in Dawlish, but lived for nearly all his life in Topsham Road, Exeter. Early commissions were as an internal decorator at Killerton House and Redhayes (now destroyed by fire). He had studied at the Exeter School of Art and later joined the staff, becoming headmaster in 1898.

He travelled widely, especially on the Continent, so Venice, the Italian Lakes and the south of France were represented in the exhibition, but the coasts of Dorset, Devon, Cornwall and Somerset seemed to be his favourite stamping grounds. He also operated a retail outlet in Catherine Street, Exeter, where hand-tinted postcards were sold. He was a well-respected local figure who had six sons and six daughters.

The only qualification for the appearance of **Henry Lamb RA (1883–1960)** in this book is on account of the oil painting he did entitled 'Military Exercise, Devonshire, 1914'. This shows several groups of soldiers in the snow beside a Dartmoor tor, and was acquired by the Royal Albert Memorial Museum in 1978. The groups of soldiers are so disposed on the canvas as to appear like boulders, and thus an extension of the tor itself.

HENRY LAMB 'Military Exercise, Devonshire 1914'. Oil on board 45 x 75cms. A cynical male reader with experience of the army will recognise the hanging about of the soldiers in the cold of a Dartmoor winter while apparently on exercises.

COURTESY OF RAMM

Lamb was associated with the avant garde movements in British art, and his picture is a world away from the Shaplands and Widgerys. He had exhibited with the New English Art Club and became a member of the Camden Town Group, a group of artists who were influenced by the Impressionist and Post-Impressionist painters. Lamb was involved with Dorelia, Augustus John's lover and second wife (see *ante*). He also painted the famous portrait of Lytton Strachey in 1914.

If the war was responsible for bringing Henry Lamb to Dartmoor, it was also the cause of **Walter R Sickert RA (1860–1942)** coming to Chagford in 1915. He would probably have gone to Dieppe, but instead came west in search of landscape subjects. Dr Sam Smiles writes in *Going Modern and Being British* (1998):

> *Walter Sickert was in Chagford in the summer of 1915, also convalescing, and there produced a number of studies of the locality. Rushford Mill on the River Teign, is close to the town and represents the one Chagford composition Sickert brought to completion as an exhibited picture, using a thickly-painted patchwork of high-toned pigment to articulate the composition as a flat mosaic of colour.*

The picture of Rushford Mill is reproduced as plate 7 in the above book, courtesy of the Fitzwilliam Museum, Cambridge. The painter was on the right bank and stepping stones lead across the Teign to the mill building in the background. A group of ducks are on the grass and doves perch on the roof ridge.

Robert James Lugg (1877–1951) was born and died in Okehampton, where for most of his life he kept a photographic and art studio and gallery in the Arcade, begun by his father. Here he sold his paintings, as well as those of F J Widgery. Lugg also sold his work through Elands of Exeter. Although tucked away below the northern tip of the moor, he gave his pictures anonymous titles such as 'A Dartmoor Stream' or 'Sheep Grazing beneath a Dartmoor Tor', which could be anywhere. Some of his work appeared on postcards published by Friths. An example of his work is reproduced in *Hidden Talents*.

Wycliffe Egginton RI RCA (1875–1951) was born in Birmingham, and educated in his home-city, Wallasey and the City School of Art, Liverpool. He was a watercolour landscape artist who painted in the style of Thomas Collier, who himself carried on the traditions of Cox and de Wint. His pictures tend to be of Ireland or Dartmoor, and he was based at various times at Newton Abbot and Teignmouth. He exhibited widely and had 11 pictures accepted by the Royal Academy. His work has a depth of feeling and quality of execution which places it above many of the paintings produced by locally-born artists.

Eustace Arthur Tozer (fl 1892–1940) may have had a Cornish connection, but so far as Dartmoor is concerned, was based in Lydford. William Crossing wrote the following about him in 1903:

> *Mr Eustace A Tozer makes a special study of sunrise effects and Dartmoor mists, and his work shows much knowledge and observation. His attention has been chiefly devoted to that part of the moor made so famous by William Widgery. His studio is close to the ancient keep of Lydford Castle, and a walk of ten minutes will take him to the commons. Being thus so happily placed Mr Tozer has opportunities for studying Dartmoor at all times and seasons, and that he has made good use of them his works amply testify.*

A watercolour of his titled 'On the Tavy at Gur Tor, Dartmoor' is a dramatic study of valley mist with the Tavy Cleave peaks rising up in the background. Two others I have seen are of 'Passing Storm, Arms Tor' and 'A River Scene, Dartmoor, with nearby squally showers'.

E A TOZER 'On the Tavy at Gur Tor, Dartmoor'. Watercolour 34 x 49cms

COURTESY J COLLINS & SON

Though he exhibited 26 times at the Royal Academy, little is known of **Bernard Cecil Gotch (1876–c.1940)**. He was born and educated in Winchester, and moved to Bath. His favourite Dartmoor territory was the River Dart.

Charles E Hannaford (1863–1955) was, according to Mallalieu, born in Liverpool. He studied in London and Paris, and later with Stanhope Forbes. But before this he worked with the borough engineer in Plymouth, before changing direction again and becoming an architect in South Wales. He made frequent sketching tours of Devon and Cornwall, and his pictures turn up in West Country auctions from time to time. I have seen examples of his work showing 'Yes Tor', 'The Road across the Moor', and a more vaguely titled work 'A Shepherd and his Sheep in a Moorland Landscape'. These fetch prices between £400 and £900. He was at one time patronised by the royal family. Later in life he lived in London and Norfolk.

Ernest William Haslehust RI RBA RWA RBC (1866–1949) – not Haslehurst as listed by Mallalieu – was born in Walthamstow and educated in Hastings, Felstead and University College, London. He painted in England and Holland, and is known as an illustrator. He provided 12 colour pictures for the 64-

page book written by Arthur L Salmon called *Dartmoor* and published – perhaps in 1913 – by Blackie and Son in their Beautiful England series. The book is curious in being typeset as if it was meant to be a large-print book for partially-sighted readers. His Dartmoor pictures do not often come on the market, but I have seen an attractive watercolour entitled 'A Shady Pool on the Dart' which sold for £1250. As I write, three of his Dartmoor images are on sale in Devon as postcards, published by J Salmon Ltd of Sevenoaks. They are of Postbridge clapper bridge, Dartmeet and one simply 'A Dartmoor Stream'.

Herbert William Hicks (1880–1944) was known as Herbie, and a studio portrait of him dressed as a country gentleman, with cap at a jaunty angle, appears on the endpapers of *Hidden Talents*. He was born in Exeter, became a self-taught artist, and painted in the style of the slightly older F J Widgery. Hicks's pictures were often sold through Samuel's Gallery in Exeter, and he was a friend of another Exeter artist, Frederick Parr (fl c.1920–1930) – see Supplementary list. A card called 'Summer on Dartmoor' by Hicks is currently on sale at the Dartmoor National Park High Moorland Visitor Centre in Princetown for £1.99.

We do not find many Cornish-based artists venturing over the county boundary to paint in Devon, but **Samuel John Lamorna Birch RA RWS RBC (1869–1955)** was an exception. When one realises he painted about 20 000 pictures in a working life of seventy years, the few Dartmoor works which come on the market are but a minute section of his output, but they are significant.

It is fortunate that we have a splendid biography to assist us – *A Painter Laureate: Lamorna Birch and His Circle* by Austin Wormleighton (Samson & Co 1995), which among its many other qualities, provides a chronology of his working life. He painted at Okehampton as early as 1903, and was still active in Devon and Dartmoor locations (not specified) right up to 1953.

S J LAMORNA BIRCH 'On the Plym at Shaugh Bridge' Oil on mahogany 25 x 35 cms (right).
COURTESY OF J COLLINS & SON

'The Heart of Devon'. Watercolour 49.5 x 59cms. Exhibited at the Royal Society of Painters in Watercolour in 1920 (opposite).
COURTESY OF J COLLINS & SON

S.J. Lamorna Birch

Birch was born in Cheshire, briefly worked in a mill, moved to Newlyn, but crossed to Paris to study and was influenced by Monet and Pissarro. He returned to Cornwall, eventually settling at Lamorna. It was Stanhope Forbes who suggested that as there was an artist in Newlyn called Lionel Birch he should call himself Lamorna Birch – and the appellation stuck.

He painted throughout Britain, the USA and the British Empire, and exhibited widely. Using either of his favoured mediums, oil or watercolour, he is noted for his brilliant technique with colour and light.

Robert Borlase Smart (1881–1947) was another artist who is best known for his Cornish pictures, though he was born in Kingsbridge in South Devon. He trained at Plymouth School of Art and the Royal College of Art, and obtained first class honours in design in South Kensington. He was then art critic of the *Western Morning News* for eleven years before heading west after 1918 and becoming one of the most active artists in the St Ives art colony. He is best known for his seascapes and in 1946 wrote *The Technique of Seascape Painting*. His oil of 'Burrator Dam' being heightened in 1928 is reproduced in monochrome in *Going Modern and Being British* (Sam Smiles edit, 1998) and is an interesting example of an artist's treatment of an industrial subject on Dartmoor. His representation of 'Chemical Works, Cattedown' is also reproduced in the same book. The originals of both are in the Plymouth City Museum & Art Gallery.

A third Cornish-based artist flirted briefly with Dartmoor. We know that **Frank Gascoigne Heath (1873–1936)** painted on Dartmoor as we have his 15 x 20.3cm oil titled 'The Quarry, Haytor, Dartmoor' as evidence, but this apart, he seems to have been a member of the Newlyn School who rarely painted outside Cornwall.

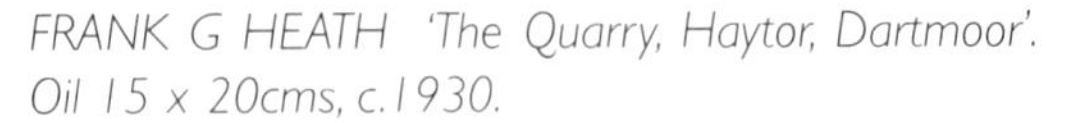

FRANK G HEATH 'The Quarry, Haytor, Dartmoor'. Oil 15 x 20cms, c.1930.

COURTESY OF HUGH BEDFORD

Heath was born in Surrey, the youngest of 12 children, and after leaving school and suffering from a chest condition, was sent to Australia on a square-rigger as an apprentice seaman on a kill-or-cure voyage. He survived this and went climbing in the Alps on his return which seems to have put an end to his bronchial problems, for he now decided to be an artist. He studied at the Academy of Fine Arts in Antwerp for two years, then returned to England and continued his studies at Sir Hubert von Herkomer's famous art school at Bushey for the full three-year course. Heath went to Cornwall in 1901–02, joined the Stanhope Forbes painting school, and here met the woman who became his wife. Although in his forties, he volunteered for the army in the First World War, but was incapacitated by a gas attack and invalided out. Back in Cornwall the Defence of the Realm Regulations prohibited artists from working out of doors, so Heath turned his hand to portraits, interiors and flower pictures. The Dartmoor work is thought to date from the late 1920s or early 1930s.

A well-illustrated privately-published monograph has been written about Heath by Hugh Bedford called *Frank Gascoigne Heath and his 'Newlyn School' friends at Lamorna.* The first edition was dated 1995, the second 2001, and the publisher is given as Frank Heath (Books and Cards), PO Box 3, Teddington.

The paintings of **Douglas Houzen Pinder (1886–1949)** and **Ben Graham (fl 1907–1930s)** seem to have been executed by the same artist – Pinder. The name Graham was used while he lived at Horrabridge. Certainly three Dartmoor views were exhibited at Elands, Exeter, in 1907 under the name of Ben Graham. These were in gouache, in the style of F J Widgery. He was born in Lincoln, and after early training as an architect became a full-time painter. After many years at Horrabridge he moved to Newquay in about 1940. He may also have painted under the name A P Shepherd. He is listed in *Hidden Talents* under both Pinder and Graham.

John Barker (fl 1920s) is a relatively unknown watercolourist, though the few examples of his work I have seen appear attractive. A bog and boulder, misty skyline picture was sold at Pyles auction rooms at Hatherleigh for £210 in 1999.

For sixty years from 1900, the Torquay-born artist **Cecil Arthur Hunt RWS (1873–1965)** exhibited widely in Britain and the USA. As a child Hunt's parents had moved to Foxworthy in Lustleigh Cleave, but he was educated at Winchester and Trinity College, Cambridge, and was called to the Bar in 1899. On his own admission he was a poor advocate, so worked in the law behind the scenes. However, his talents lay elsewhere, and he travelled widely, wrote for various journals, used Foxworthy as his country studio in the summer, and immersed himself in the life of the area, even producing a one-off book called *My Saxon Farm: The Story of Foxworthy* in 1941 for family retention.

It was hardly surprising that as his artistic fame increased he left the law and began painting full time. He was a climber too, contributing to *The Alpine Journal* and visiting Norway, Switzerland, Scotland, Ireland, Wales and the Lake District. He also found time to go to Italy, Greece, Spain, Holland and the USA.

Macmillan commissioned him to provide the frontispiece illustrations in 1927 for the Widecombe edition of Eden Phillpotts's 20 Dartmoor novels, though the sepia result is hardly representative of Hunt's usual Turneresque technique. In 1996 an exhibition of his work was held by Chris Beetles, and the excellent catalogue gives numerous examples of his work as well as photographs of his life.

CECIL HUNT The frontispiece of Eden Phillpotts's novel The Beacon *(Widecombe edition (1927–28 no 16 of 20 volumes). Cosdon Beacon in the background; mine workings, possibly Ramsley Mine, in the foreground.*

AUTHOR'S COLLECTION

CECIL HUNT 'Swaling on Dartmoor'. Watercolour and body colour 22.8 x 30cms. This is the practice of burning off the vegetation, particularly the heather, to improve the grazing. The white patch on the right is probably a china clay quarry. Hunt painted a number of pictures of china clay workings throughout his life.

COURTESY OF CHRIS BEETLES LTD

Cecil Hunt was unusual. Artists who have painted Dartmoor have either been home-grown and stayed in the county or visited Devon from outside. Hunt became internationally known while retaining his links with the moor.

There lived at Dean Prior for thirty years – from 1919 to 1949 – one who earned his living as a commercial artist, **James Thorpe (1876–1949)**. He is not known as a Dartmoor artist, but painted a fine series of watercolours portraying the houses in his parish as they were in the 1930s and 1940s which are in a private collection and occasionally on view. He had a hand in the stained glass window erected in Dean Prior church in 1926 in memory of the Reverend Robert Herrick.

Thorpe earned his living by contributing sketches and cartoons to *Punch* and other journals, wrote for *Country Life*, illustrated several books, and wrote three which he illustrated himself: *A Cricket Bag* (1929), *Phil May: Master Draughtsman and Humorist 1864–1903* (1932) and his autobiography *Happy Days* (1933) which is packed with his drawings and watercolours (reproduced in monochrome). A delightful book, and little known.

His studio was brought down by train from Esher, where it had belonged to John M Swan RA pre 1919. Thorpe wrote of it in 1933 as follows:

> *Its discordant ugliness has by length of association been gradually forgiven and it has served its purpose as a workshop ever since. Sometimes in the fierce gales it creaks ominously, but so far it has stood up stoutly – and I am touching wood.*

It still stands behind the cottage where he lived, and now does duty as the parish hall!

Andrew Beer (1862–1954) was another commercial artist, but he worked in a different field. His full name was William Andrew Edward Beer and he was born in Exmouth. *Hidden Talents* gives 21 lines to his life and work. So far as Dartmoor is concerned he is best known for a slim paper-covered book of 16 hand-coloured sepia pictures published in Bristol c.1910 called *Gems of Dartmoor*. Sets of his postcards are also known (see pages 63 and 64). He was an illustrator for a firm of printers in Bristol for much of his life.

Harry (or Harold) Sutton Palmer RBA RI (1854–1933) – who always signed his work Sutton Palmer – was another artist who is best known now as an illustrator. A & C Black published a thin book of his pictures in 1926 called *Devon Water-Colours*, but of the 20 views, only three were of Dartmoor, and the captions simply identified the image. Mallalieu gives him 12 lines, stating that his style is 'traditional and technically very accomplished'.

The 1920s and 1930s saw the merging of art and graphic design. In 1922 the first Ordnance Survey one-inch tourist map of Dartmoor was published. The cover, with art deco calligraphy and a painted moorland landscape of nowhere-in-particular, by **Arthur Palmer (1875–1947)** is an attractive composition. The Ordnance Survey's own book, *Map Cover Art*, written by John Paddy Browne and published in 1991, is a useful guide to the history of this byway of graphic design, and brings the subject up to the date of publication.

The railway posters of the era are now collectors' items. A semi-abstract design of a road undulating across a plain landscape was executed by **E McKnight Kauffer (1890–1954)** for the Great Western Railway in 1932 and is now in the Victoria & Albert Museum. It was displayed in the *Thirties Exhibition* at the Hayward Gallery in 1980, and bears the legend in large capital letters GREAT WESTERN TO DEVON'S MOORS. McKnight Kauffer came to England from America in 1914 and became a highly successful commercial artist – a worker of miracles, in sales terms.

In this summary of 1930s design it must be mentioned that F J Widgery also produced posters for the Great Western Railway. Commercial work was carried on from his studio across the road from the Royal Albert Memorial Museum. He died in 1942, so his passing and the intervention of the Second World War are major interruptions in the story of Dartmoor art. (See page 51.)

Jumping ahead to the 1950s, the traditional, naturalistic way of producing pictures for the railway was revived in the early post-war years, and one of the artists commissioned by British Railways was **Jack Merriott VPRI ROI RSW (1901–1968)**. His fine watercolour of Widecombe-in-the-Moor of 1954 was reproduced in hundreds of railway compartments, and the story is well told in *Landscapes under the*

JAMES THORPE John Full, or Old Jan, as Thorpe wrote in his 1933 autobiography Happy Days, *one 'of the old school of farm labourers'. He lived at Dean, near Buckfastleigh, all his life, had started work at seven years old, and never went in a train. By his feet is the wooden keg of cider he took to work which he could empty in one draught. Pen and ink 6 x 6cms.*

AUTHOR'S COLLECTION

Luggage Rack by Greg Norden (GNRP 1997), and the picture reproduced therein. His 'Storm over Dartmoor' is in the Royal Albert Memorial Museum, Exeter.

During the course of a life devoted to painting, whether by teaching, writing about it, or actually doing it, Merriott travelled throughout Britain, and was eventually severely injured when returning to his home in Sussex after giving an art demonstration at Killerton House, near Exeter. His car skidded on black ice, and he received injuries from which he never recovered.

E MCKNIGHT KAUFFER 'Great Western to Devon's Moors'. Kauffer's progressive poster designs did not always find favour with the GWR management, but this 1933 poster is regarded as a classic.
COURTESY OF SCIENCE & SOCIETY PICTURE LIBRARY

1945 to the present day

The Second World War and its aftermath stifled creative endeavour of many kinds on Dartmoor. Apart from the fact that people had other things on their minds, for several years much of the open moor was barred to visitors while intense training was carried on. Only gradually did things begin to return to normal. The artists particularly affected by this exclusion were those in their middle and possibly most productive years.

Judith Ackland (1898–1971) was born in Bideford and trained in her home town and at Regent Street Polytechnic in London. Here she met Mary Stella Edwards, with whom she developed a partnership which took them to the Lake District, Wales and Yorkshire. They used as a studio 'The Cabin', a small hut perched beside the slipway at Bucks Mills. Ackland also painted on Dartmoor, and an example of her work done in 1956 of 'Hexworthy Bridge' is in the Royal Albert Memorial Museum in Exeter. But the best place to see examples of her work is at the Burton Art Gallery, Bideford, where there are more than 40 of her pictures, though only a few of these are of Dartmoor. One of them is called 'Looking off the Moor' and has Dartmoor in the foreground. It is on sale at the Burton Art Gallery as a postcard.

A contemporary of this artist was **Sheila Hutchinson (1906–99)** who was also a lifelong resident of Bideford, though she was born in Weare Giffard, not far away. Despite the distance from Dartmoor she drove long journeys, sometimes on her motorbike, to reach her painting destination. I have seen competent watercolours by her of 'Brent Tor' and 'Scorhill Circle' in a private collection. When she died she left a legacy worth around £100 000 to the Burton Art Gallery, which was named after her school friend Mary Burton, who died in her forties.

Stanley Roy Badmin (1906–1989) is included here only on the strength of one picture we know he painted of Dartmoor, of the Ockery Bridge, just east of Princetown. Badmin was a most prolific artist and illustrator, and was involved in the wartime *Recording Britain* project. But it was during the years following the Second World War that he made his name as one of those who revived interest in the countryside. A splendidly illustrated book *S R Badmin and the English Landscape* (Chris Beetles, 1985) ably rounds up many of his most important works.

S R BADMIN 'Clapper Bridge, the Ockery', Princetown. Watercolour 20.3 x 27.9cms. Exhibited at the 1968 RWS autumn exhibition. Great Mis Tor is just visible in the far distance, top left, between the foliage.

COURTESY OF CHRIS BEETLES LTD

Dartmoor only began to attract sculptors when **John Skeaping RA (1901–80)** first came to the area in about 1937 with Morwenna, his second wife. (His first wife was Barbara Hepworth.) They stayed at Creaber Cottage, Gidleigh, and Skeaping, always a keen horseman with a penchant for animal paintings and carvings, took at once to the freedom of Dartmoor. He wrote in his autobiography *Drawn from Life* (Collins 1977): 'Life on Dartmoor was bliss. It provided me with everything I wanted…'

JOHN SKEAPING 'Akua-ba' 1931, acacia wood, 1.1m high, with 'Memorial', granite 1955–56, 1.98m high, in the background. This was carved in memory of his son Paul.

PRIVATE COLLECTION

His first commission to work in granite was a pair of giant tortoises, each 76 x 137cms for a children's settlement in Sussex. The blocks of stone came from Blackingstone Quarry, and they were carved at Bert Grattan's yard at Sticklepath, but to 'cut his teeth' on granite, and to 'play himself in' as it were, Skeaping produced a 1.06m torso from a piece of rock found for him on the moor by a workman he refers to as 'Old Stony Adders'. This torso is still on Dartmoor in a private collection, as is the 2m-high free-standing granite male figure he carved in 1955/56 as a memorial to Paul, the son of John Skeaping and Barbara Hepworth, who was killed in an air crash in Malaysia in 1953. Although Skeaping had no interest in posterity, it was this *tour de force* which he cared for most, because of the craftsmanship which went into the carving.

The Skeapings established themselves at Puggiestone, at Leigh Bridge near Chagford, after the war. The house was large, with room for a nursery for their small children, a studio, kennels for Morwenna's standard poodles and John's greyhounds, and stables for the horses.

Towards the end of his life he moved away from England, to Mexico and the Carmargue, and here he concentrated on wonderful lively drawings, pastels and gouaches of animals, mostly horses. Some pastel drawings exist of Dartmoor ponies.

In June 1991 a retrospective exhibition of his work was staged at Ackermann's Gallery in New Bond Street, London, and it showed him to be a man of enormous talent in a variety of materials. The full-colour exhibition catalogue *John Skeaping 1901–1980 A Retrospective* illustrates his many skills and tells much about his life, with photographs from the family albums of him at work on Dartmoor.

The moor has not attracted many sculptors. Perhaps the granite is too intractable a material, though stone can be imported as Peter Randall-Page is doing at the present time. Skeaping sculpted in wood as well as granite. It may be that the weather-sculpted shapes of the tors, dry-stone walls and tortured trees restrain the artist from competing with these natural forms.

Clifford Ellis (1907–85) and **Rosemary Ellis (1910–)** were the married couple who collaborated in designing about 100 jackets for the Collins 'New Naturalist' series of books between 1945 and 1982, and as this included the *Dartmoor* volume, we include them here. By using a single team of able artists to produce the whole run of jackets the publishers achieved a consistency of quality and unity of design, rare in marketing.

Francis Goodchild ARCA (1904– ?) was for a time head of Plymouth Art College. He had an impressive list of exhibitions to his name, and perhaps one of the last was in August 1971 when he had a show at Chagford Galleries. His paintings are traditional in style, and I have seen examples of 'Easdon Tor' and 'Rippon Tor'. For a time he lived at Churston Ferrers, near Brixham.

Another professional art teacher who painted Dartmoor was **Clifford Fishwick (1923–97)**. He came to Exeter in 1947 as painting master at Exeter College of Art, and was appointed principal in 1958, retiring in 1984. His heroes were Cézanne and Turner, and he sought to extend the tradition of English landscape painting into modern terms, thus his work tended towards abstraction. His Dartmoor paintings are not numerous as he preferred seascapes.

CLIFFORD & ROSEMARY ELLIS Book jacket designed by the husband and wife team who did so many jackets for the New Naturalist series. This was for the Harvey & St Leger Gordon volume of 1953.

AUTHOR'S COLLECTION

Marjorie Holland (fl 1959–) is the most senior of the artists whose work was described by Jenny Pery in her paper to the Devonshire Association at its Millennium Conference. (See the *Transactions* of the Devonshire Association, volume 132, 2000). She has lived in Plymouth since 1959, and produces abstract landscapes based on field and moorland patterns.

Michael Honnor (1944–) has the distinction of having had a £25 book published by the Antique Collectors' Club in 2000 about his work. He lives and works on the moor above the Erme, north of Ivybridge, and his favourite areas to paint are on the rivers Erme, Dart and Bovey, though in recent years he has travelled to Scotland, Ireland, Cornwall and Suffolk. He has undertaken commissions for a long list of financial institutions, and British embassies and high commissions abroad. He was one of the artists invited to take part in the exhibition *New Inhabitants: Seven Artists on Dartmoor*, which was shown at the Royal Albert Memorial Museum in Exeter in 1993. Water, especially running water, is inspirational for him, and his home patch, where fields and woods merge into the open moor, has been a fruitful source of imagery. For many years he has run the Dartington Print Workshop. (For further details see the *Transactions* of the Devonshire Association, Volume 132, 2000.)

MICHAEL HONNOR The artist at work (above). *'Dartmoor – Blackthorn Hedge, April'* (right). *Oil on canvas 73.6 x 86.3cms.*

COURTESY OF ARTIST

MICHAEL HONNOR 'River Coming into Sunlight' (left). *Oil on paper 83.8 x 74.9cms. 'Dartmoor Shallow River, May'* (above).

COURTESY OF ARTIST

Philip James (1948–) made his first painting of Dartmoor on a visit in 1967 though his first efforts hardly impressed fellow students at the Slade School of Art where his tutor commented, 'I suppose it gets you into the fresh air.' But the moor remained 'under his skin' so that he has returned time and time again. Every four months he visits Haytor and, using the area as a base, sets out to explore the ever-changing features of the moor, revisiting favourite spots such as Black Down, Sheepstor, Haytor Vale and Manaton, but always finding something new to say. He no longer completes canvasses on site, choosing rather to capture his vision using watercolours or by making small drawings to build up to oils in his Teddington, West London, studio. James states that it is 'like a filtering process', there's a sense of a conversation with a gradual revelation of the subject.' It does not worry him that he is working some 200 miles away from his subject.

PHILIP JAMES 'Haytor Vale' (top). *Oil on canvas 61 x 91.4cms. 'Saddle Tor'* (above). *Oil on canvas 40.6 x 51cms. 'Buckland Woods'* (right). *Oil on canvas 76 x 91.4cms.*

COURTESY OF ARTIST

Graham Griffiths (1951–) is an artist who had become studio-bound until his love affair with Dartmoor began on a hot August afternoon on a trip with his two daughters to Vixen Tor. There he was transfixed by the sight of a plume or aura of violet-green light rising from the granite, an experience shared with his daughters but not captured by his camera. Thus he was fired to return to the moor again and again on a quest to capture this weird phenomena, one that began to show itself to a greater or lesser degree at many other tors and stone circles. These often exhausting route marches into the wilderness, getting lost in mires or fog, had the effect of stripping away thirty years' worth of self-confidence and skill, yet rendered him a clean slate, which he feels allowed him to paint like never before. He will trudge miles with the weight of 500 mahogany-encased pastels on his back, often painting long after moon rise.

GRAHAM GRIFFITHS 'The Bowerman in Spring" (below). *Oil pastel on paper 69 x 48cms. 'Lints Tor'* (below left). *Oil pastel on paper 48.8 x 71.7cms.*
COURTESY OF ARTIST

Reg Lloyd RI (fl 1970 –) is an artist who tries to bridge the gap between painting and sculpture. Some of his works have abstract foregrounds and representational backgrounds. His studio is in Bideford. He had a major exhibition at Chagford Galleries in August 1973.

Alan Richards (1932–) is probably best known as a Dartmoor painter for his picture of 'Powder Mills Farm' done in 1972 which is available in Exeter as a postcard, and has been used on a local calendar. He has lived in Exeter for many years, but Dartmoor is only a small part of his colourful corpus of work.

ALAN RICHARDS 'Powder Mills Farm, Dartmoor' Oil. Painted c.1972. Colour screenprint.

COURTESY OF RAMM

Edward Burra (1905–76) came to Dartmoor in September 1973 with his sister Anne and friend William Chappell, when they stayed at Tavistock and drove round the moor from there. He is not known as a landscape painter, being more inclined to reflect urban scenes or distorted humanity, but towards the end of his life he made car-borne forays all over England, Wales and Scotland, favouring the undeveloped countryside. His method of working was not to paint, sketch or even take photographs in the field, but to memorise the scene which he would paint back in the studio. Hence the viewer should not attempt to identify the watercolour captioned simply 'Dartmoor' done in 1974, and available from the Royal Albert Memorial Museum as a postcard.

The semi-humorous Dartmoor-like picture of three enormous lorries grinding up a road resembling Widecombe Hill was in fact of a hill near Buxton in the Peak District and executed in 1970. Both pictures are illustrated and commented upon in the catalogue to the Hayward Gallery exhibition of 1988, called simply *Edward Burra* (Arts Council of Great Britain).

EDWARD BURRA 'Dartmoor'. Watercolour executed in 1974, derived from a motoring holiday based at Tavistock in September 1973. This would have been painted in his studio using his memory of the moor.
COURTESY OF RAMM

KEN HOWARD *'The Old National School, Sampford Spiney'. Oil on board. Undated but c.1980.*
COURTESY OF ARTIST

Perhaps the best-known living artist connected with Dartmoor is **Ken Howard RA RWS NEAC (1932–)**. He used the Old School House at Sampford Spiney as a studio for eighteen years, specifically, he wrote in his delightful book *Inspired by Light: A Personal View* (David & Charles 1998), 'so that I could paint the snow in winter'.

Howard initially came to the West Country as a Royal Marine, and his first exhibition was at Plymouth Art Centre in the 1950s. After demobilisation he returned to London, where he was born, and did three years at the Royal College of Art. When he acquired his studio on Dartmoor he was quoted in the *Western Morning News* (15 March 1976) as saying:

> *I think Sampford Spiney will change my work. People who have seen the paintings for the exhibition say it's very different. The moor has got a thing about it that finally must affect anybody that lives on it. I love the quiet, the loneliness, if you like. In London you can feel a sense of being alone. But when on the moor there's no sense of that. You're only lonely when there are others to feel lonely against.*

Since then he has travelled throughout the world, and has a studio in Mousehole, Cornwall. He is President of the New English Art Club. A Sampford Spiney snow scene has been used by the Royal Academy for one of its Christmas cards.

Simon Thomas (1960–) is a sculptor who contributed to the 1989 exhibition at Plymouth City Museum & Art Gallery entitled *The Fabricated Landscape: Dartmoor*. He produced seven balls of Merrivale granite, each individually carved, and laid them in a line, perhaps like a prehistoric stone row, but the stone evoked the tors and the line of stones suggested a river. The exhibit was titled 'Erme'. Thomas was also commissioned to produce sculptures for the Common Ground land art project which became known as *New Milestones*. He produced four grains of wheat in oak which were sited on coastal pasture at Bat's Head, near Lulworth. Each 'grain' is about the size of a sheep.

Simon Lewty (1941–) is best known for his contribution to the exhibition entitled *The Inspiration of Landscape: Artists in National Parks* (Phaidon 1989). He had visited Dartmoor as a child, and decided not to revisit it, but to recycle his memories of visits many years previously. His response was a long panel (58 x 213.3cms) bearing a series of pictorial images and recollections, loosely woven into a vague route.

Brendan Neiland RA (1941–), an exact contemporary of Lewty's, made a considerable impact at the same exhibition with his large (129.5 x 182.8cm) oil on canvas called 'Dartmoor skyscape across Gidleigh Common 1988'. This threatening view, with dark clouds occupying the top third of the canvas, and a black silhouetted tor-studded skyline running along the bottom of the picture is very powerful. He said at the time that although he mostly lives and works in London, this commission to paint Dartmoor had given him a new love in his life. In 1998 Neiland was elected Keeper of the Royal Academy Schools.

BRENDAN NEILAND *'Dartmoor Skyscape across Gidleigh Common'. Oil on canvas 1988. This is possibly the largest painting represented in this book – 129.5 x 182.8cms. After visiting the moor, and taking photographs, it took Neiland five weeks in his London studio to create the painting* (opposite).
COURTESY OF ARTIST

Chris Chapman (1952 –) has established himself in the twenty-five years he has lived on Dartmoor as a deeply sensitive photographer, who has produced an extensive archive of images recording local life in all its forms. Spilling over from this have been other commissions, as presenter of open-air television programmes (including Exmoor), photographic work on the Somerset Levels, and pictures for guide-books. But Dartmoor is his home and his workshop. His studio is at Throwleigh. His art has been exhibited widely in Britain and the USA, and his magnificent volume *Wild Goose & Riddon* (Halsgrove 2000) shows that not only can he take evocative and timeless photographs, but he can write good prose also. His documentary chapter recording the last days of the Dennis family at Truelove Farm has one reaching for the tissues.

A co-operative work he achieved with others, notably the sculptor Peter Randall-Page (see *post)* is *Granite Song* (Devon Books 1999) and shows his ability to work with other artists. Jenny Pery wrote about his work in the *Transactions* of the Devonshire Association, Volume 132, 2000.

CHRIS CHAPMAN *'Dawn from Hound Tor', 1977* (above). *'Drystone walling on Teignhead Newtake', 1981* (right). *Chris is not related to the Dawlish firm, Chapman & Son.*

COURTESY OF CHRIS CHAPMAN

Peter Randall-Page (1954–) is internationally known as a sculptor and has been based at Drewsteignton since 1987. He seems not to find his provincial domicile a handicap as commissions come in from far and wide. He has made his mark on Dartmoor by producing a number of works which have been introduced into the local landscape with the greatest of care for the environment. They seem to add rather than detract from their surroundings, when one comes across them, unsigned and unlabelled.

Most of these have been sponsored by the national charity Common Ground, and were written up in *Granite Song* (see *ante*). The sculpture which gives the book its name lies on a small island in the River Teign, and is a large roughly egg-shaped boulder split in half, a coiled pattern exposed to view. A somewhat similar sculpture, called 'Passage' stands at the top of a ragged beech avenue and astride the entrance to an enclosure within Whiddon Deer Park. This pair of sculptures has the coiled pattern filled with lead. Jenny Pery wrote about his work in the *Transactions* of the Devonshire Association, Volume 132, 2000.

PETER RANDALL-PAGE *At work in his studio at Vete Mill farm, Drewsteignton* (left). *'Passage' 125 x 163 x 119 and 125 x 163 x 127cms* (above).
PHOTOGRAPHS BY CHRIS CHAPMAN

Dartmoor was an important element in the life of **Stuart Armfield (1916–99)** particularly during his later years. He had moved to Plymouth from Looe in 1980, and, as Robert Earl wrote in an article about him in the *Western Morning News* of 21 January 1992, 'He now revels in the outdoors of Dartmoor where he travels to sketch and photograph the images created within that wilderness for development in his studio.' Stuart Armfield was quoted thus, 'I feel those responsible for Dartmoor are not doing a bad job, for I find so much endures, even the lanes that I have known on its edges for so many years.' He went on to say that he respected the work of the earlier Dartmoor painters, like the Widgerys.

Armfield began his working life as an assistant art director at Ealing Film Studios, but a change of direction after the Second World War when his Quaker background forced him to register as a conscientious objector, found him taking on commissions from international institutions and industry. Among these was a painting for Robert Maxwell, and Armfield's work 'Vortex' which hangs in the United Nations building in New York.

His range of work was incredibly wide, for in addition to landscapes he painted birds, animals, marine subjects and portraits. He exhibited at the Royal Academy and the Royal Watercolour Society, and in 1977 the Plymouth Art Gallery held a retrospective exhibition.

Richard Long (1945–) is regarded internationally as one of Britain's most important artists. In 1989 he was awarded the Turner Prize for his contribution to British art. His work defies classification, but could be termed land art with a theatrical content. For inspiration he has been to the Sahara, Japan, Morocco, Alaska, Bolivia and nearer home to Scotland, Ireland, Dorset and Dartmoor – a favourite location. Some of his productions are sculptures, some are mud works, and some come as framed objects.

His 'A DARTMOOR WALK. EIGHT DAYS ENGLAND 1987' was done for the 1988 'Artists in National Parks' project. It consists of a line traced on a large piece of paper above a cryptic 18-line log or diary, part of which reads, in capital letters, '...TO MOONLIGHT TO DRYING THE TENT TO TAW HEAD TO EAST DART HEAD TO A CLOUD BURST…' This panel has been exhibited at the High Moorland Visitor Centre at Princetown since it opened in 1993.

Some works are more sculptural, and 'Turf Circle' is one of these. The interested reader is referred to his book *Walking in Circles* published in 1991 by the South Bank Centre. The German-published guide, but available in English, *The West Country* by Peter Sager (Pallas Guides 2000) has a lengthy section on Richard Long, and his 'SIXTY MINUTE CIRCLE WALK ON DARTMOOR 1984' is reproduced on page 161.

John Virtue (1947–) is another artist with strong Dartmoor associations who is given a lengthy write-up in Peter Sager's German-published guide *The West Country* (Pallas Guides 2000). It contains a colour photograph of him in his studio.

After studying art at the Slade in the late 1960s he taught art briefly in Liverpool before moving to Green Haworth near his childhood home of Accrington. It was while he was working here that he developed his individual style of landscape art in black and white in a variety of materials. He moved to South Tawton in 1987 where he lived for eight years before moving to Exeter where he concentrates on the Exe Estuary. In January 2001 he had an exhibition at the Tate St Ives in which he showed the largest paintings ever exhibited in the gallery, and described by the *Western Morning News* reviewer as 'awe inspiring'. He has exhibited frequently in the USA and has an international reputation as a landscape artist. His work was illustrated in the exhibition *New Inhabitants: Seven Artists on Dartmoor* held at the Royal Albert Memorial Museum, Exeter, in 1993. Jenny Pery wrote about his work in the *Transactions* of the Devonshire Association, Volume 132, 2000.

The name Collier has already been mentioned in this book in the person of Arthur Bevan Collier on page 60, and **Nicholas Collier (1947–)** is the latest, and a contemporary member of the family, to qualify as a Dartmoor artist.

He is currently head of art at Kelly College, Tavistock, which he reached by way of Exeter College of Art and teaching jobs in Dorset and Africa. His oil on paper of 'Sweltor Quarry' was a chosen exhibit at the first open exhibition of the South West Academy of Fine & Applied Arts held in Exeter in 2000. Jenny Pery wrote about his work in the *Transactions* of the Devonshire Association, Volume 132, 2000, and she illustrated her essay with his painting, reproduced in monochrome, of an oil on canvas of 'Merrivale Quarry'.

Alan Lee (1947–) is an artist who lives on Dartmoor, in Chagford, but whose *metier* is the study and representation of mythology, legend and the stories of Tolkien. His career followed a similar course to that of **Brian Froud (1948–)** who also lives in Chagford parish. They both find the in-country of Dartmoor enormously inspirational to their art.

BRIAN FROUD 'Oak Tree Man'.

COURTESY OF ARTIST

Perhaps Froud's images are more faery-like, while Lee's are representational of the characters he is illustrating. Neither of them consciously copy the landscape they see around them, but they have to admit that it motivates their work which has moved on since they shared a studio in London's Soho.

Alan Lee was the first to move to Chagford, but Brian Froud came soon after and bought a house outside the town. Their first collaborative publication was *Faeries* in 1977 which became a great success with 600 000 copies sold in nine languages by 1984 (*The Dictionary of 20th Century British Book Illustrators* Alan Horne, ACC 1994). *Faeries* is still in print all these years later. Their careers have progressed with both doing film work with the Monty Python genius Terry Jones. Another well-known artist with whom Froud collaborated was the late Jim Henson of Muppets fame.

Recently Lee was conceptual artist and set decorator of the film of *The Lord of the Rings*. He has also illustrated *The Mabinogian* and *Merlin Dreams* and was awarded the Carnegie Medal for his edition of *The Iliad*. Froud's most recent work was *The Faeries' Oracle* and he was the subject of an eight-page article in the December 2001/January 2002 edition of *Devon Today* by Guy Cracknell which is illustrated by numerous Froud pictures.

We are fortunate that soon after his death the story of **Ernest Knight (1915–95)** was told by Biddy Shillito in her eponymous book published in 1997 (Chapel Publications), and this included numerous illustrations, many of them in colour.

Like Gaul, his life was divided in three parts. His childhood and early years were spent in England, and he studied at the Chelsea College of Art. He went to South Africa in 1938 and stayed there more or less continuously until 1956 doing a variety of jobs, mostly associated with art. On returning to England he and his wife initially settled in Brixham, but moved to a house on Widecombe Hill in 1978, and here they stayed until his death, though they travelled a great deal on the Continent. Much of his work is oil on canvas and is traditionally representational. He was a kind, friendly man, always eager to talk about his art and give time to others.

Harry Scott (1954–) is a photographer who first came to public notice so far as Dartmoor is concerned in the exhibition organised by Plymouth City Museum & Art Gallery in 1989 called *The Fabricated Landscape; Dartmoor,* and which generated a catalogue of the same name.

He favours black and white images, and if his pictures at first seem to lack human interest, one realises that most have some object which owes its origin to man's intervention on the moor. Thus one finds the Haytor granite tramway, leats, mining remains, plantations and field boundaries. His skies, filled with cloud contrasts, more than hold their own above the bleak and damp landscape below.

Michael Morgan RI (1928–) is an East Devon watercolour artist who includes Dartmoor among his subjects. Other areas he visits are Tuscany, Wales, the Lake District and the coast.

He came to painting after a career in education, and his first solo exhibition was in 1991. Since then his work has been greatly in demand, and he now holds annual exhibitions at the Marine House at Beer. He is a founding academician of the South West Academy of Fine & Applied Arts. Perhaps it is his adventurous approach to composition combined with his very distinctive use of colour which makes his work so remarkable.

When asked what inspires him he replied:

> *A list must include the work of other painters whose work I admire, the encouragement of those who enjoy my work, the impact of a stunning view and the thrill of the unanticipated. I believe too that it is important to have technical competence and a command of the medium. My challenge is to find new and personal ways of expressing what I want to say in paint. I read a lot, visit galleries a great deal and have studied the development of watercolour painting in a systematic and thorough way.*

He was then asked what are his favourite subjects:

> *My particular interest is in trying to capture the drama and mood of the landscape and I paint little else. I am intrigued by the desolate mountainous regions of Snowdonia and the Lake District, the bleakness of Dartmoor, the vast golden vistas of Tuscany and winding paths that lead to remote buildings.*

Richard Dack is an artist who taught for twenty-two years at Kingsbridge Community College, travelled – to Iceland, Africa and Australia – and now works in a variety of materials – paint, ink, chalk, sometimes looking for a collage texture. He exhibits through Cove's Quay Gallery, Salcombe, and had two mixed-media pictures accepted for the first (2000) open exhibition of the South West Academy of Fine & Applied Arts. One of these was 'Fernworthy Relics', and the piece that Jenny Pery wrote about him in the *Transactions* of the Devonshire Association, Volume 132, 2000 was illustrated by his 'Dartmoor Snow' (Huntingdon Warren) reproduced in monochrome.

MICHAEL MORGAN 'Dartmoor edge – a remote Dartmoor farm', 2000. Watercolour 33.8 x 43.9cms.
COURTESY OF ARTIST

Stephen Woods (1929–) is a documentary photographer of the first order, a modern day Robert Burnard. In 1988 Devon Books published his *Dartmoor Stone* – reprinted by public demand in 1999 – which was a joyous celebration of the granite he has been photographing for much of his adult life.

He was born in London, but during National Service he learned his profession as a photographer, and later taught his skill to students in Southampton. His mother, Iris, lived in Widecombe-in-the-Moor for the last thirty years of her long life, so during frequent visits to the moor he built up an archive of photographs of stone artefacts, stone buildings and stone walls.

Two further books have been compiled by Stephen in recent years, *Widecombe-in-the-Moor: A Pictorial History of a Dartmoor Village* (Devon Books 1996) and *Uncle Tom Cobley and All: Widecombe-in-the-Moor* (Halsgrove 2000).

STEPHEN WOODS 'Teignhead farm gateway'. Woods's Dartmoor Stone *is a lifetime's record of photographing granite artefacts with informative captions. This type of gate employed individual bars, five in this case. The left-hand post has L-shaped slots. Most similar pairs of posts still surviving on the moor have been set farther apart to permit the passage of modern machinery, and are fitted with conventional gates. The hinges are shown here, but the gate is missing. They could date to 1790 when the farm was built.*

Two photographs by Stephen Woods (opposite) *show Saddle Tor and water cascades on the River Yealm. The latter photograph was used on the reprint of* Dartmoor Stone *(Devon Books, 1999).*

PHOTOGRAPHS BY STEPHEN WOODS

Lee Pengelly (1970–) is a photographer who has spent all of his life in Plymouth, with Dartmoor 'on the doorstep', but feels that his real interest in the moor was born, along with his passion for photography, six years ago. From what he recalls as a 'disastrous' first outing into landscape photography, his work has been increasingly sought after for use in a number of regional publications, as well as books, postcards and calendars. He sums up the moor's inspiration thus:

> *Dartmoor has everything a photographer could dream of, tors, rivers and vast untamed landscapes. Photographers always talk about 'the light', I'm no exception, for me Dartmoor is unbeatable in this respect. The glow and the warmth of the light bring out all the textures of the moorland and granite. Add this together with the unpredictable weather and you have all the elements for great photographs.*
>
> *I often visit the same scenes each year and on every occasion the weather and the light have completely transformed them. But for me the best aspect of Dartmoor has to be its timeless quality, each photograph is unaffected by modernity, very few places can boast this now.*

LEE PENGELLY 'Princetown Church, Dartmoor' (right) *and 'Dartmoor ponies, Nr Princetown, Dartmoor'* (opposite).
COURTESY OF PHOTOGRAPHER

David Bellamy (1943–) was born in Pembrokeshire, and studied life drawing in Hampstead for several years. In 1986 he wrote and illustrated *The Wild Places of Britain* (Webb & Bower) with chapters on the remoter parts of England, Wales and Scotland, adding his own narrative to the watercolours which illustrate the book. He began his Dartmoor chapter with the words, 'Nowhere have I experienced such a strong feeling of the ancient past than on Dartmoor,' and his images have captured the brooding atmosphere of which he writes.

He found that 'Dartmoor is perhaps at its best in foul weather…', and some of the experiences he relates of attempting to paint in windy, wet weather show why so many artists do sketches on the moor and complete the picture in the studio. He has subsequently written and illustrated *The Wild Coast of Britain* and *Painting in the Wild.*

Lady Elizabeth Kitson DL SEA AFAS came to painting after a career as a well-known rider also involved in showing, point to pointing, hunting and showjumping and instructing. Her work draws on both her surroundings and her former career; using oil, watercolour and pastels, she considers movement and light to be the essence of her work, focussing on people, animals and landscapes. She is a member of the Society of Equestrian Artists and Armed Forces Art Society and works mainly to commission. These include in the UK, 'Dartmoor 2000', 'River Tamar Fishing Maps', military portraits, the Royal Yacht *Britannia*, Christmas cards for the British Horse Society and famous horses. She was recently appointed Deputy Lieutenant.

ELIZABETH KITSON 'Looking across the Walkham valley'. Oil on board 38 x 55.8cms (right). *'Moorland Stream'. Watercolour 22 x 15cms* (opposite).
COURTESY OF ARTIST

E. Kitson

Ray Balkwill (1948–) is a versatile Exeter-born artist who paints Dartmoor and estuary views. For many years he worked in advertising, and became a professional painter in 1990. He has diversified from watercolours into mixed-media, pastels and oils, and works from a studio in Exmouth. His paintings have been accepted by the Royal Institution of Painters in Watercolours at the Mall Galleries, London, and the Royal West Academy. In the South West Academy of Fine & Applied Arts open exhibition in 2000, he was joint prize-winner for the most popular painting voted by the public, and in 2001 he was runner-up. He describes his feelings for Dartmoor thus:

> *I have always been drawn to the vast open spaces, big skies and changing moods of Dartmoor. My childhood was spent at Okehampton and the feelings I have for the northern edge of the moor are special to me. As a child, places like Belstone, Yes Tor and Sourton were my playgrounds and the freedom, mystery and unpredictability have stayed with me ever since; particularly the tumbling waterfalls and boulder-strewn rivers which are now my favourite subjects to paint. Trying to capture the elemental forces in nature have long been an inspiration to my work and I am a strong advocate of painting en plein air. To paint Dartmoor well, one has to understand it – to 'live' the moor. This is why painters such as Widgery are unsurpassed masters. Like them, I strive to capture the mood, atmosphere and a sense of place.*

RAY BALKWILL 'Sunlight and shadow, Dartmoor' (right) *and 'Waterfall on the East Dart'* (opposite). *Both mixed media 35.5 x 53.5cms.*

COURTESY OF ARTIST

Carol Ballenger is probably best known for the book she produced jointly with John Powls, *Dartmoor Dreams: Poetry and Photography of Dartmoor* (Devon Books 1995). She took the photographs which encapsulate in its 36 pages all that is best about Dartmoor – the rocks, space, antiquities, vegetation and running water. She has had another book *Stone Universe* published by Halsgrove (late 2001), also a co-operative effort with the poet John Powls, which extends to 120 pages. She came to Devon in 1980 after several years as a professional musician, and lives in a village near south Dartmoor. Jenny Pery wrote about her art in the *Transactions* of the Devonshire Association, Volume 132, 2000.

CAROL BALLENGER 'Daffodils and bracken, Horrabridge' (top), *'Beech leaves, Dunsford Wood'* (above) *and 'Haytor from Smallacombe Rocks'* (right).
COURTESY OF PHOTOGRAPHER

Mark Gibbons (1949–) was born in Lyme Regis, and obtained a degree in psychology, but his heart was set on painting as a career. However, he first travelled to the USA, Australia and the Far East before returning to Europe by the Trans Siberian Railway. He now lives in Ashburton. He is self-taught as an artist. In 1999 Bossiney Books published *Mark Gibbons's Dartmoor*, an attractive book of 20 of his watercolours, reproduced in A4 size, and each with an extended caption. His publishers have followed this book with another, *Mark Gibbons's The South Devon Coast.*

MARK GIBBONS 'Clearing Mist, Tavy Cleave'. Watercolour, 31.5 x 44.6cms.

COURTESY OF ARTIST

Lawrence Freiesleben (1962–) was born in London of German parents. His art education was one term at Amersham Art College, where his introduction to the work of Paul Nash was his main benefit. Since then he has travelled around England, settling north of Crediton where he finds the proximity to Dartmoor stimulating. He says that his abstract paintings in oils or watercolours are modified by his moods and the weather. Jenny Pery wrote about his work in the *Transactions* of the Devonshire Association, Volume 132, 2000.

Lionel Aggett RIBA (1938–) is a case of local boy makes good, as he was born at Whiddon Down, on the north-eastern edge of Dartmoor, though he now lives at Crediton. He trained and worked as an architect until 1991, when he became a full-time professional painter. He gets much of his inspiration these days from southern European countries, as he finds the light so helpful. He was quoted in the *Western Morning News* on 21 January 2000 as follows:

> *The character of the place or scene is ultimately defined and enhanced by the ever-changing light. For a painter, an understanding of light is fundamental. One of the main challenges is to capture whatever light one is confronted with.*

He now sets off with his artist wife Anne in their camper van for weeks at a time, returning with a stack of portfolios ready for framing. He uses pastels, oils, acrylics and watercolour, though he finds pastel suits his preference for painting on site. He has written and illustrated a number of how-to-do-it books on painting techniques. He exhibits widely, and had a painting accepted at the first exhibition of the South West Academy of Fine & Applied Arts in 2000.

LIONEL AGGETT 'Winter, Dartmoor'. Pastel 25 x 32.5cms. Panorama across north-east Dartmoor (right). *'Headland Warren, Dartmoor'. Pastel 25 x 3.25cms* (opposite).

COURTESY OF ARTIST

Graham Ovenden (1943–) has painted Dartmoor during his years of living near Bodmin, so may be counted as a landscape painter, though his portraits of young girls, his photography, and his diversion into architecture by designing and building his fantasy home, the eccentric neo-Victorian Gothic extravagance known as Barley Splatt, mark him out as a polymath of unusual versatility. He is a founding academician of the South West Academy of Fine & Applied Arts.

As a 12-year-old boy he built a harpsichord, and now includes musicianship and composing among his many accomplishments, along with poetry and writing. His painting has led him and his wife Annie to come together with other like-minded artists – the Arnolds, the Peter Blakes and David Inshaw – to found the Brotherhood of Ruralists as an exhibiting group. Clearly they follow in the wake of William Blake, Samuel Palmer, the Brotherhood of Ancients and the Pre-Raphaelites. Five of Ovenden's Dartmoor pictures are reproduced in the monograph *Graham Ovenden* published by Academy Editions in 1987, the work of several authors. The paintings are not location specific, but convey the moorland atmosphere in mystical terms.

OVENDEN 'Dartmoor evening', 1984. Oil on canvas (above), *'Towards the sea', 1990. Oil on panel* (right) *and 'Spoil tips', 1982. Oil on panel* (far right). *Three pictures executed by the artist since the 1980s.*
COURTESY OF ARTIST

Like Ovenden, **Stephen Braund** lives and works in Cornwall, where he is an artist and illustrator teaching at Falmouth College of Arts. He also owns the Atlantic Press, a private publishing enterprise which in 1998 brought out a delightful hardback book *Something Amiss on the Moor.* The picture 'Up along the Parapet' which was accepted for the 2000 open exhibition of the South West Academy of Fine & Applied Arts was one of the illustrations in this book. Stephen writes that '…the book tells a peculiar story of a journey across the moor of three gypsy children, where things are not always quite as they seem.'

STEPHEN BRAUND 'Up along the parapet'. The reader will note 'the observer' beneath one of the arches…

COURTESY OF ARTIST

Trevor Felcey (1945–) moved to Throwleigh in 1987, so is a neighbour of Chris Chapman who took the photograph of Felcey painting one of his figurative works near his home. Before settling in Devon he trained at Camberwell School of Art and the Royal College. As Jenny Pery hints in her paper on contemporary artists in the Devon landscape in the *Transactions* of the Devonshire Association 2000, his discovery of a certain oak tree in Whiddon Deer Park was almost a life-changing experience. He returned to it again and again and it is reproduced in monochrome to illustrate her article.

TREVOR FELCEY The artist painting in Balls Field, Throwleigh, 1990.

PHOTOGRAPH BY CHRIS CHAPMAN

GARRY FABIAN MILLER 'The Enclosure'. The artist standing within his sculpture below Parke, Dartmoor National Park Authority HQ, in 1992.

PHOTOGRAPH BY CHRIS CHAPMAN

Rosalind Pierson is a landscape miniaturist who lives near Wells, but spends a good deal of time on western Dartmoor producing her tiny pictures of the moor. They may only measure 8.2 x 5cms but they are accurate as images of Dartmoor both in details and colour. Her work has won many awards since 1973 and is regularly accepted by the Royal Academy. She has exhibited in London, the USA and France.

Garry Fabian Miller (1957–) was born in Somerset but moved to Devon in 1988, now living in Manaton. His work is as varied as his skill is versatile. In 1991 he organised a sculpture with £12 000 worth of sponsorship which involved the building of five concentric timber circles, the largest 56ft across, in the meadow below Parke, the Dartmoor National Park headquarters. Jenny Pery in her paper in the *Transactions* of the Devonshire Association 2000 describes how in 1989 he composed a photogram of beech leaves gathered daily and assembled into a picture of the genesis of change brought about by photosynthesis.

Robin Armstrong (1947–) is known as an angling artist, but has recently diversified – how otherwise could he have completed a watercolour and pen painting which was accepted for the 2000 South West Academy of Fine & Applied Arts open exhibition titled 'Desert Sunset'? His entry for the 2001 exhibition was the bronze sculpture of a shark.

He made his name with his first book *The Painted Stream*, which became a bestseller, and since then has produced several more and illustrated others. For fifteen years he was a water bailiff on the River Walkham, so he knows western Dartmoor well. He now works from his Kingfisher Studio, near Lopwell at the foot of the River Tavy.

ROBIN ARMSTRONG 'Singing wren' (above). Graphite on paper 15 x 25cms. 'Out of the forest' (right). *Oil on canvas 45.7 x 71cms.*

COURTESY OF ARTIST

ROBIN ARMSTRONG 'Goldeneye, rare visitor on the Plym' (top). *Watercolour 25.4 x 38cms. 'Rainbow trout, escaped, migrated and returned'* (bottom). *Watercolour and acrylic 40 x 72.3cms.*

COURTESY OF ARTIST

Mary Gillett is an artist and printmaker based on western Dartmoor who has a deep feeling for the landscape which gives her such inspiration. One of her images was reproduced in colour in the 2000 brochure for the *Nine Days of Art* festival, and Jenny Pery wrote about her work in the *Transactions* of the Devonshire Association 2000.

Dominic Welch is a sculptor in stone who learned his trade with Peter Randall-Page, but who has now set up on his own. He still lives and works in the parish of Drewsteignton, but from a different group of farm buildings. Like Randall-Page he prefers to work in Kilkenny limestone, a material which has to be imported from the Republic of Ireland. Granite is a coarser stone which demands a different technique. His finished objects tend to be organic shapes owing more to nature than to human or industrial concepts. A two-page illustrated article about his work by Philip Knowling appeared in *Dartmoor: The Country Magazine* issue no 9, summer 2000.

DOMINIC WELCH 'Twinned' 1999. Ancaster weatherbed, 55 x 50 x 27cm (above). *'Unfurling' 1997, Kilkenny limestone, 115 x 110 x 15cm* (right).
COURTESY OF ARTIST

Mairi Laing Hunt grew up studying wildlife, and sculpting in natural clay dug from beds near her remote childhood home. Her talent was recognised by a company specialising in high-quality figurines and at 17 she was offered a three-year apprenticeship which included time to study life-sculpture at Aberdeen School of Art. When at the end of it she met her husband-to-be, the grandson of the twentieth century watercolourist Cecil Hunt, her artistic career might have seemed set fair. Instead it has had to be worked around travelling the world with her husband, working in a variety of farming jobs and eventually helping to run the couple's own farm at Neadon on the eastern edge of Dartmoor, along with bringing up two small children. Despite such demands, Mairi has continued to create her stunning, often life-sized pieces, successfully, developing a style along the lines of the freer, less commercially-constrained, style she aspires to. Though still much involved with the farm and family life, she is now able to work from her own studio. Private commissions include large animal sculptures for individual clients and smaller gallery pieces including deer, hounds and other animal studies, as well as a series of limited edition artworks commissioned by Halsgrove Fine Art.

MAIRI LAING HUNT Applying the finishing touches to the clay model (above) *and the completed work in its natural parkland setting* (left).

COURTESY OF ARTIST

Justin Knowles (1935–) is a self-taught Exeter-born artist who did not start painting seriously until he was thirty but whose career since has brought him international renown. In the 1960s he had work in major exhibitions: The English Eye, Marlborough Gerson 1965, The New Generation, Whitechapel Art Gallery, London 1966, New York City Art Gallery 1967, and others. He was the major prize-winner in the Arts Council of Northern Ireland painting competition 1966, and won the first prize in the Paris Biennale 1967. His work is represented in many public collections, including the Tate in London, and several private collections.

After losing all his major work in a fire at his studio, he left Devon for a time, along with painting and sculpting, though continuing to draw. But around fifteen years ago, he returned to Bovey Tracey, achieving a considerable output of work in both two and three dimensions.

His sculptural work using stainless steel, glass and other materials containing pigment, is uncompromising, whilst his drawing is equally sparing of line. The view from his home looks out across the uncluttered vista of Dartmoor, and as fellow artist Jane Beeson comments, 'it is this sense of space, spatial relations and the pattern in between that is the all-pervading quality of Justin's work'.

JUSTIN KNOWLES Stainless steel with circular forms and space: simulated in Dartmoor landscape from Art-form concept 1996.

COURTESY OF ARTIST

Martin Proctor (1942–) lives in Ipplepen, near Newton Abbot, and following a career involved in architecture and building restoration has now thrown himself into watercolour painting which he combines with his love of the countryside and country walking. He never uses a camera and is constantly sketching.

In the summer of 2000 he had a successful exhibition at the Marine House, Beer, of the paintings he executed as a result of his walk along the Mariners' Way, from Dartmouth to Bideford. A number of those were of Dartmoor sites, and included Dunstone, Lettaford and Kes Tor.

Susan Derges (1955–) is based in her studio/gallery in South Zeal, and from here produces her photograms. These nature-induced patterns come about by shining light through the object on to photosensitive paper. She moved to Devon in 1992, following a thorough training in art at Chelsea School of Art, a British Council scholarship in Berlin, two years at the Slade and a year in Japan. Jenny Pery included her work in the paper about Dartmoor artists in the *Transactions* of the Devonshire Association 2000.

Carol Banks lives and works in Gunnislake, on the borders of Devon and Cornwall. She is unusual in using batik to portray riverscapes, but also paints with acrylic, produces screen prints, and both representational and abstract wall hangings. She has had numerous exhibitions, and her work is widely collected in Europe and North America.

Veronica Gould is a textile artist who grew up in Patagonia. Since coming to live in Devon in 1990, the landscape of Dartmoor has become the driving force of her inspiration. Her work explores and reflects the colours and shapes of the changing seasons, and particularly the hidden landscape of undergrowth, ferns, lichen, streams and bridle paths. Veronica has arrived at a technique that draws on the English tradition of woven tapestry and the ancient oriental art of painting on silk, using dyes on thick silk to build up a series of layers, creating subtlety and depth. Much of her work is in the form of wall hangings but she also hand paints scarves, cushions and fabric.

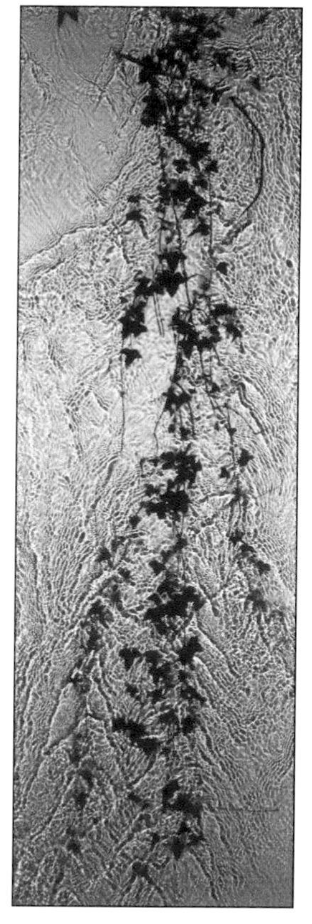

SUSAN DERGES 'Ivy – the River Taw'. Cibachrome photogram 167 x 60cms.

COURTESY OF ARTIST

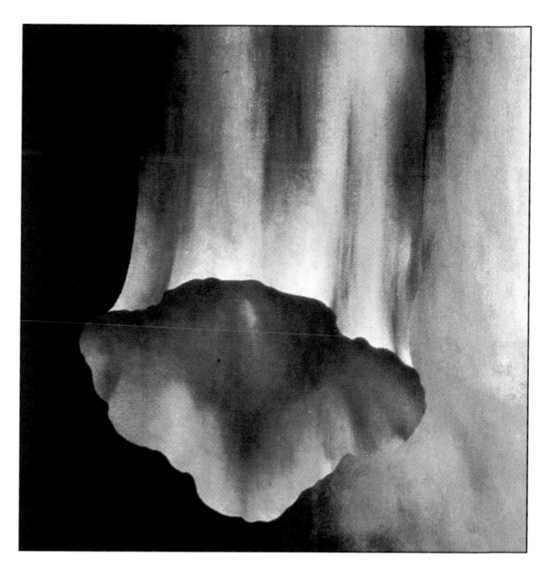

VERONICA GOULD Two wall-hanging examples 150 x 90cms (left) and 80 x 80 cms (right).

COURTESY OF ARTIST

JENNY PERY 'Haytor Rocks'. Lithograph on paper 11 x 23cms, used as an invitation to an Aune Head Arts function at Parke.

AUTHOR'S COLLECTION

Jenny Pery's paper on Devon artists in the *Transactions* of the Devonshire Association for 2000 has been frequently referred to. She compiled that paper as a contemporary art critic, though she is a painter and printmaker herself. Her introduction 'set the scene', with a brief outline of Devon's place in art during the last hundred years. I hope this book will go some way towards consolidating the picture.

Certainly the art scene in Devon and on Dartmoor in particular is exceedingly healthy at the present time. I could have mentioned many more active artists in my survey, though some are included in the Supplementary list. As I write, the second annual open exhibition of the South West Academy of Fine & Applied Arts is pulling in the crowds at two locations in Exeter. This is a major new event in the country's art calendar, including as it does the West Country.

In 2000, in the middle of September, a more local festival called *Nine Days of Art* was enjoyed over all of Dartmoor and much of South Devon. This celebration of the visual arts involved 180 participants at 67 venues and encouraged the public to visit the artists in their studios and workplaces. *Nine Days of Art* received extensive sponsorship and a well-produced 36-page brochure helped visitors find their way around. It was not intended to be an annual event. Over the last twenty-five years we have seen a significant number of artistic initiatives on the moor come and go, including the Bellever 3D (TSW) sculpture project which comprised large works set in the forest.

In 2001 the artists and craftsmen of Chagford organised an exhibition trail over several days in July, and there was the usual summer *Mythic Gardens Sculpture Exhibition* at Stone Lane Gardens not far away.

Most Dartmoor towns and villages now have commercial galleries, and annual exhibitions are held by local art clubs and associations. I have not felt able to comment on the music arena, but the Ten Tors Concert Orchestra has had sell-out concerts, and the Dartmoor Folk Festival centred on South Zeal is a regular feature of the summer season.

In June 1997 Aune Head Arts was formed as a not-for-profit company dedicated to charitable purposes. It is a community-based body fired with creating new and challenging art through collaboration with individuals and organisations. As this book goes to press, Moretonhampstead's Dartmoor Flight Public Arts Trail is complete and ready to follow. A 16-page booklet, available locally, explains the route and describes the artists' contribution. The Dartmoor art scene is truly flourishing.

Supplementary list of artists associated with Dartmoor

ABDEY, Mark	*1968–* Contemporary.
ACKERMAN, Arthur Gerald RI	*1876–1960.*
ALLOM, Thomas FRIBA	*1804–72* See Mallalieu.
ALTHOUS, Fritz B	*fl 1881–1914* See Mallalieu.
ANDERSON, John	*fl 1876* Painted 'Holystreet Mill, Chagford' in 1876.
ARCHER, Peter	See *Transactions* of the Devonshire Association 2000 Contemporary.
BANKES, John	
BARCLAY, T H	*fl 1860–70* Watercolourist.
BARLOW, John Noble ROI	*1861–1917* Several paintings in Plymouth Art Gallery (Newlyn School).
BARR, Joyce	Twentieth century.
BAWDEN, Edward CBE RA	*1903–* Watercolour artist and illustrator.
BELL, A C	Briefly mentioned in *Crossing's Dartmoor Worker.*
BIRKMYER, James B	*fl 1868–98* Occasional painter on Dartmoor.
BOWING, L	*fl 1910* Mentioned in *Hidden Talents.*
BRADSHAW, Dorothy	*1897–* Lived at Budleigh Salterton.
BRANSCOMBE, George G	*1887–1960* A 1931 watercolour of Dartmeet is known showing both bridges.
BRANWHITE, Charles B	*1851–1929* See Mallalieu.
BULGIN, C	Exh'd *1907* Has four lines in *Hidden Talents.* A painting titled 'Sheep and Yes Tor' is known.

CAUNTER, Henry	Nineteenth century. Lived in Ashburton. Painted Abraham Cann, wrestler.
CHARLTON, G	*fl 1920–30.*
CHRISTIAN, John	Provides watercolour holidays on north-east Dartmoor.
CLEMENT, Professor Robert OBE	Has concentrated since 1978 on painting the landscape near Great Sherberton on central Dartmoor. See also *Landscapes; The Artists' Vision* by Peter Howard 1991, fig 108.
COAD, James	*fl 1930* See *Hidden Talents.*
COLLIER, R P	Later Lord Monkswell, brother of A B Collier. Mentioned in *Crossing's Dartmoor Worker.*
COLLINS, William RA	*1788–1847* A painter of landscapes and genre scenes who travelled widely around the British Isles and the Continent, and who may have painted in Devon. His 'Rustic Civility' (oil on canvas 1833) is in the V & A, and on show in the British Galleries, 2002. He was the father of the writer Wilkie Collins.
CONDY, Nicholas Matthews	*1816–51* Better known as a marine painter, but RAMM has watercolours of the Ivybridge and Slade railway viaducts.
COOK, Samuel NWS	*1806–59* See Mallalieu. Briefly mentioned in *Crossing's Dartmoor Worker.*
COTTIS, Sally	Contemporary. See c/v in South West Academy of Fine & Applied Arts catalogue for 2000.
COX, Stanley	*fl 1930s.*
CURNO, John	Contemporary photographer, living in Drewsteignton, who takes photographs of local life in the manner of Chris Chapman. See *Drewsteignton – a portrait of a Dartmoor Parish* (Halsgrove 2001).

DADD, Frank RI	*1851–1929* Draughtsman and painter, favoured the River Plym.
DAMPIER, Arthur	*fl 1866–75* Known to have lived and worked in Holloway, London.
DAWSON, Alfred	Illustrated books of J L W Page.
DEAKIN, Peter	*fl 1855–79* See Mallalieu.
DEAN, Roger	Executed the sparrowhawk sculpture in Moretonhampstead
DES CLAYES, Alice	*fl 1930s* Painted horses.
DINGLE, Thomas	A father and son. Possibly both Thomas, who painted landscapes. See Mallalieu.
DUNNING, John T	*1851–1931* An oil painter who frequently painted Dartmoor *(1916–30)*.
ELLIOT-REEP, Tracey	Contemporary. Photographer. Has published a small book of photographs called *Dartmoor.*
FARQUHARSON, David ARA ARSA RSW	*1840–1907* Landscape painter in oil and water-colour who visited Dartmoor in 1892. Mentioned in Mallalieu.
FELIX, N	Known to have painted Okehampton Castle and Berry Pomeroy as a pair.
FOSTER, Myles Birket	*1825–99* Peter Howard includes a picture (fig 40) in his *Landscapes: The Artists' Vision* which may be Holy Street Mill.
FOWERAKER, A Moulton	Went to Exeter School and is known to have painted moorland scenes.
FRIEDENSON, Arthur A	*1865–1955* Represented in Burton Art Gallery, Bideford. Known to have painted on Dartmoor.

GAINSBOROUGH Thomas RA	*1727–1788* He visited Devon, and stayed with William Jackson, Exeter cathedral organist, composer of secular songs, and painter of the Devon landscape. He is thought to have visited the Teign valley, possibly with his friend and host.
GALLWAY, D P	Twentieth century.
GASTINEAU, Henry G OWS	*1791–1876* This prolific artist is not known as a Dartmoor painter, but he did show a painting titled 'Near Buckland-in-the-Moor, Devon' at the Royal Watercolour Society exhibition of 1832.
GEAKE, Frances Mary Eleanor	*1903–55* Lived at Newton Abbot and Exeter. Painted in watercolour throughout Devon, and on Dartmoor, exhibited at the Royal Academy.
GODDEN, Ernie	*1946–* Exhibits at Lion House Gallery, Moretonhampstead and Chagford Galleries.
GOULD, Alexander Carruthers RBA	*1870–1948* Lived and worked in Porlock, Exmoor, but sometimes painted on Dartmoor. Two of his Exmoor paintings are reproduced, in monochrome, in *An Endless View.*
GRANT, James Y	*fl 1827–41* Did oil paintings of Dartmoor.
GUILLE, J D	A signed and dated, '64, picture titled 'Spooners and West Dartmoor Hounds on the slopes of Peak Hill' was sold at Bearne's in September 1991.
HARRIS, Arthur Wolsey	A watercolour titled 'Monolith near Dartmoor, Chagford district' with four others, was sold at Bearne's in Sept 1991.
HARRIS, Kevin	*1957–* Exhibition at Wadebridge, Cornwall, in May 2001.
HATCH, Frances	*1955–* Based in Dorset, but executes non–topographical works of Dartmoor uplands. Exhibits at Alpha House Gallery, Sherborne.

HAYES, Claude RI	*1852–1922* Sometimes known as Charles. Mallalieu writes of him at some length.
HEAD, F G	*fl 1827–45* Not much known about this artist.
HIDER, Frank	*1861–1933* Has a 14-line entry in *Hidden Talents*. A fanciful view of 'The Devil's Bridge, Dartmoor' sold for £650 in 1999.
HOOK, James C RA	*1819–1907* See Mallalieu. Thought to have been in Chagford in 1857.
HOUSDEN, Penny	Contemporary. Pen and ink artist who drew the pictures which comprise *Down Dartymoor Way* (1990). Her mother, Mary Housden, wrote the text.
HOWARD, E D	Probably Evelyn, who lived in Exeter before moving to Northam in North Devon in 1902. Painted on northern Dartmoor, but there is a c.1930 oil of 'The Dart near Eagle Rock' in Torre Abbey, no 241 in the catalogue.
HUGHES, Eleanor RI	*1882–1959* A member of the Newlyn School who occasionally painted on Dartmoor.
HUNT, William Holman ARSA RSW Hon RWS	*1827–1910* Major pre–Raphaelite painter. Was in Ivybridge in 1860.
JEFFERY, Emmanuel	*1806–74* Born in Exeter and painted West Country scenes. There are eight Exeter subjects in the RAMM, but he is known to have painted on Dartmoor.
JENNISON, Robert	*1933–* East Devon artist who occasionally paints/draws Dartmoor.
JUTSUM, Henry	*1816–69* Visitor to Devon, and Dartmoor, between 1836 and 1861, when he favoured the River Erme area. Latterly painted in oils. Mentioned in Mallalieu.

KANGIESSER, H F

A painting titled 'Leistley Craig, near Moreton Hampstead, North Devon' was shown by this artist at the Royal Watercolour Society exhibition in 1814.

KEMP–WELCH, Lucy RBA

1869–1958 An accomplished artist who specialised in painting horses. She visited Exmoor more than Dartmoor with other sporting artists – Cecil Aldin, Sir Alfred Munnings and Lionel Edwards. A Dartmoor picture in coloured chalks of a mare and foal called 'Dwellers on the Moors' is reproduced in Laura Wortley's *Lucy Kemp–Welch 1869–1958, The Spirit of the Horse* (ACC 1996.)

KRAUSS, Amy Elizabeth

Exhibited at the Royal Academy between 1907–15.

LAWRENCE, John

Contemporary. Exhibition of his paintings at Exeter Cathedral Chapter House in August 2001. See *Western Morning News* 10 May 2001.

MACE, John

Painting at Torre Abbey, 226 in catalogue, watercolour titled 'New Bridge, Dartmoor' c.1946.

MERIVALE, John Herman

1799–1844 Friend of Francis Towne. See entry in Mallalieu.

MITCHELL, Alfred

According to Mallalieu, was a marine painter living in Plymouth, but a painting called 'End of Moor' is known.

MOORE, Henry RA RWS

1831–95 Visited northern Dartmoor and River Dart during *1856–69*. Lengthy reference in Mallalieu.

MORTIMER, Lewis

fl c.1920–30 see reference in *Hidden Talents* to T Mortimer and possibility of confusion.

MOSER, Rosemary

Contemporary South Devon artist who wrote in the *Nine Days of Art* brochure (2000) that she is 'currently working in oils and making prints on the moods and seasons of Dartmoor…'

MULLER, William James

1812–45 Visited Chagford area in the 1840s. Lengthy entry in Mallalieu.

MUNNINGS, Sir Alfred KCVO PRA RWS RP	*1878–1959* Known to have passed across Dartmoor and is thought to have painted gypsies en route. Preferred Exmoor.
NEATBY, Edward Mossforth RMS ARCA	*1888–1949* Occasional visitor to Dartmoor. Known to have painted 'An afternoon at Fingle Bridge'. His wife has an entry in *Hidden Talents*.
NEAVE, David S	*fl 1903–36* Exhibited extensively, including at the RA. Lived in Topsham in 1911. An evocative watercolour of 'Cranmere Pool' is known.
NEVITT, Diane	Contemporary. Favours abstract landscapes. See *Transactions* of the Devonshire Association, 2000.
NEWMAN, Arthur	A gouache painting 'On the Okement, Dartmoor' is known.
NEWMAN, Beryl (nee Trist)	A picture titled 'Spring evening – Widecombe-in-the-Moor' dated 1953 is known.
OYSTON, George	*c.1860–c.1918* Known to have painted on Dartmoor. *Hidden Talents* gives him three lines.
PARR, Frederick	*fl c.1920–30* Friend of H W Hicks. See *Hidden Talents*. Tended to paint northern and eastern Dartmoor.
PARTIS, Richard	Contemporary. A painting of a National Trust holiday cottage in Drewsteignton, used as a National Trust Christmas card, is known.
PASCOE–HOLMAN, Edwin Charles BWS	*fl 1918–39* Usually painted in watercolour. Pictures of Bellever, Widecombe and near Lydford are known.
POPKIN, G P	*fl 1850–59* May have lived in Wales, Exmouth and Bath. Pictures of Dartmoor watermills are known. See Mallalieu.
SAUNDERS, Charles L	*fl 1884* An artist of this name who died in 1915 is given four lines in Mallalieu. A signed watercolour

dated 1884, titled 'Old Mill, Chagford near Exeter' was entered in Bearne's auction for October 2001, with an estimated price of £400–£600. This is likely to be Holy Street Mill.

SCHREIBER, R C A — An oil of 'Wallabrook clapper bridge, Dartmoor' was entered in Fenner's auction of March 1993.

SMITH, Claire — Contemporary.

SNELL, Frederick John — *1862–1935* Artist and author who lived at Tiverton. Wrote 16 books according to Brockett's *Devon Union List* (1977). See entry in *Hidden Talents*.

SOPER, Thomas James — *c.1815–82* Worked on and around Dartmoor 1837–69, where he favoured the River Dart. See Mallalieu.

SPOONER, Molly — *Died 1998* Painted on western Dartmoor.

STARK, James — *1794–1859* Norwich School artist. See Mallalieu for lengthy entry. Bearne's sold his 'Fishermen by a wooded stream' in October 1999 which could be of Dartmoor. Estimated price of £10 000–£15 000.

SWEET, Walter Henry — *1889–1943* Studied at the Exeter School of Art under his friend John Shapland. Not known as a Dartmoor artist, but they occasionally turn up. See *Hidden Talents*.

SYER, John RI — *1815–85* One of the local pioneers of Dartmoor painting. See *Crossing's Dartmoor Worker*. See also *A Vision of Dartmoor* by Jane Baker, and Mallalieu.

TADD, Kenneth — *fl 1980s–1990s* Watercolour artist based in Bristol who took up full-time painting and teaching after 1982.

TALFOURD, Field — We have only the briefest reference to this artist, in *Crossing's Dartmoor Worker*.

TREVOR, G — *fl 1920s–30s* See *Hidden Talents* – eight lines.

TRICK, Edward William — *1902–91* Born in Exeter. See *Hidden Talents* in which there is a reproduction of a painting of his of Lynmouth.

TURNER, Edward — Exhibition of 70 semi–abstract watercolours, mostly of Dartmoor subjects, at the RAMM in September 1992. See the *Western Morning News* 18 August 1992.

UNWIN, James — *fl 1836–71* Oil painter. At Chagford 1871.

UPHAM, John William — *1772–1828* A pupil of Francis Towne, and there is a pencil and sepia watercolour in the RAMM 'Okehampton Bridge'. See Mallalieu.

WALMESLEY J — See figure 31 in Peter Howard's *Landscapes: The Artists' Vision.*

WALTERS, George Stanfield — 1838–1924 Worked on Dartmoor *1892–1912*. See lengthy entry in Mallalieu.

WARD, James RA — *1769–1859* See lengthy entry in Mallalieu. Painted the River Erme.

WATTS, Frederick Waters — *1800–70* Watercolourist. Worked in South Devon and favoured the River Dart. Five lines in Mallalieu.

WEBB, Ernest George — *1876–1951* Represented in Plymouth Art Gallery. See *Hidden Talents* 14 lines and a picture of Buckland-in-the-Moor.

WELCH, Margaret Kemp — Little known. A pair of small watercolours was sold by Phillips in July 1991 titled 'Wallabrook, Dartmoor' and 'A Babbling Brook and Rustic Gate'. Estimated price £200–£300. No connection with the sporting artist Lucy Kemp–Welch is known.

WESTWOOD, Norman — Contemporary. Lives in South Devon. Paints semi–abstracts of Dartmoor.

WHITE, John RI	*1851–1933* Painted in oil and watercolour. Lived latterly in East Devon but painted occasionally on Dartmoor. An oil titled 'Down from the Hills: the Okement at Cullever Steps' is known, also others of northern Dartmoor.
WHITE, Melville L	*fl c.1900* One of six sons of John White RI. 'A Dartmoor Stream' is known.
WHITWORTH, Terry	*1949* Contemporary. Lives in Dorset, but exhibited a watercolour of 'Hound Tor, Dartmoor' at the South West Academy of Fine & Applied Arts open exhibition 2000.
WIDGERY, Julia	Older sister of F J Widgery. Exhibited between 1872–80. A pair of Dartmoor oils was for sale at Godolphin Fine Art, Chagford in October 2001 for £1495. Mallalieu gives her two lines.
WILLIS, John H	*1887–1950s* Oil and watercolour artist who favoured eastern Dartmoor.
WORTHINGTON, Robert A OBE FRCS	*1877/8–1945* Exeter surgeon and amateur artist. Watercolourist. Painted on Dartmoor and in East Devon. Represented at RAMM but not with a Dartmoor picture.

Bibliography

ANON	*Illustrated Catalogue of Pictures and Sculpture in the City Art Gallery.* Royal Albert Memorial Museum, Exeter 1926.
ANON	*Loan Collection of Works by Early Devon Painters Born Before the Year 1800.* Royal Albert Memorial Museum, Exeter 1932.
ANON	*Exeter Museums Bulletin No 44.* Royal Albert Memorial Museum, November 1978. Contains several paragraphs about the acquisition of a painting by Henry Lamb 'Military Exercise, Devonshire 1914'.
ANON	*The Burton Art Gallery and Museum Catalogue.* Burton Art Gallery & Museum, Bideford 1996.
ANON	Auction and sale catalogues, many illustrated, extending back to 1988, for: Bearne's, Brookside Fine Arts, Christie's, J Collins & Son, Greenslade Taylor Hunt Fine Art, Marine House, Mill Gallery, Phillips, Walker Galleries, Sotheby's.
BAKER C Jane	*Paintings and Drawings by Francis Towne and John White Abbott.* Exeter Museums Publications No 57 1971.
BAKER C Jane	*William Widgery and Frederick J Widgery.* Exeter Museums Publication No 66 1872. Exhibition catalogue.
BAKER C Jane	*Paintings of Dartmoor: Eighteen-Twentieth Century Work.* Exeter Museums Service 1985. Exhibition catalogue.
BAKER C Jane	*A Vision of Dartmoor: Paintings by F J Widgery 1861–1942.* Victor Gollancz 1988.
BAKER C Jane	*A Vision of Dartmoor: Paintings and Drawings by William Widgery and F J Widgery.* Exeter Museums Service 1988. Exhibition catalogue.

BAKER C Jane — *Devon Life* May 1988. 'A Tale of Two Widgerys'.

BAKER C Jane (compiler) — *Catalogue of Oil Paintings, Watercolours, Drawings and Sculpture in the Permanent Collection 1978.* Exeter Museums Publication No 93 Royal Albert Memorial Museum, Exeter 1978.

BAKER C Jane & ACLAND, Anne — *Portrait of Devon – Killerton House.* The National Trust. Exhibition catalogue 1976.

BEETLES, Chris — *S R Badmin and the English Landscape.* William Collins 1985.

BELLAMY, David — *The Wild Places of Britain.* Webb & Bower/Michael Joseph 1986. Contains a chapter 'Bog–trotting on Dartmoor' illustrated by the author's watercolours.

BOYLAN, Patrick J — *Robert Burnard's Dartmoor.* Exeter Museums Publication No 62 1972. Exhibition catalogue.

BURNARD, Robert — *Dartmoor Pictorial Records.* Privately published.

Vol 1	1890	150 copies
Vol 2	1891	200 copies
Vol 3	1893	200 copies
Vol 4	1894	200 copies

BURNARD, Robert — *Dartmoor Pictorial Records.* Devon Books 1986 facsimile edition.

BURY, Adrian, RWS — *Francis Towne: Lone Star of Water-Colour Painting.* Charles Skilton Ltd 1962.

BURY, Adrian, RWS Edit. — *The Old Water-Colour Society's Club Sixtieth Annual Volume.* Bankside Gallery 1985. Contains articles on Edward Duncan and Ken Howard.

BUTLER, Simon — *Dartmoor Century: Photography on Dartmoor Across a Hundred Years.* Halsgrove 2000.

CARRINGTON, N T — *Dartmoor: A Descriptive Poem.* John Murray, Second Edition 1826.

CHAPMAN, Chris — *Wild Goose & Riddon: The Dartmoor Photographs of Chris Chapman.* Halsgrove 2000.

CHUGG, Brian	*Devon: A Thematic Study.* Batsford 1980. Contains a chapter 'Devonian artists and their work'.
COLE, Beverley & DURACK, Richard	*Railway Posters 1923–1947.* From the collection of the National Railway Museum, York. Lawrence King Publishing 1992.
COMMON GROUND Various Authors	*Granite Song.* Devon Books 1999. The Dartmoor sculptures of Peter Randall-Page.
CROSS, Tom	*The Shining Sands: Artists in Newlyn and St Ives 1880–1930.* Westcountry Books/Lutterworth Press 1994.
CROSSING, William	*Crossing's Dartmoor Worker.* David & Charles 1966. A reprint of 1903 newspaper articles in The *Western Morning News.* The chapter on 'The Artist' is relevant.
CROSSING, William	*Crossing's Guide to Dartmoor.* Peninsula Press 1990. This edition has colour illustrations by P G Stevens on the cover and inside.
GIBBONS, Mark	*Mark Gibbon's Dartmoor.* Bossiney Books 1999.
GRANT, Col M H	*A Chronological History of the old English Landscape Painters (in oil).* F Lewis, eight volumes, revised edition 1957–71.
GRIGSON, Geoffrey	*Britain Observed: The landscape through artists' eyes.* Phaidon 1975.
GRUNDY, C Reginald Edit.	*The Connoisseur: An Illustrated Magazine for Collectors* (Vol 65 January–April 1923). Contains an article about Samuel Prout.
GUNNELL, Clive	*My Dartmoor.* Bossiney Books 1977. Contains a chapter 'The Painters of Dartmoor'.
HAMILTON–LEGGETT, Peter	*The Dartmoor Bibliography 1534–1991.* Devon Books 1992.
HEMERY, Pauline	*The Book of Meavy: Dartmoor parish, village and river.* Halsgrove 1999.
HEMMING, Charles	*British Landscape Painters: A History and Gazetteer.* Victor Gollancz 1989.

HONNOR, Michael — *Michael Honnor Paintings.* ACC 2000.

HORNE, Alan — *The Dictionary of 20th Century British Book Illustrators.* ACC 1994.

HOSKINS, W G — *Devon* Collins 1954.

HOUFE, Simon — *The Dictionary of 19th Century British Book Illustrators and Caricaturists.* ACC 1998 revised edition.

HOWARD, Ken — *Ken Howard: A Personal View – Inspired by Light.* David & Charles 1998.

HOWARD, Peter — *Landscapes: The Artists' Vision.* Routledge 1991.

HOWARD, Peter — *Historical Atlas of South-West England.* 'Early tourist destinations; the influence of artists' changing landscape preferences'. Kain and Ravenhill, edits, University of Exeter Press 1999.

HOWARD, Peter — *Landscape Research* (Vol 4, no 3 autumn 1979). 'The use of Art Works in Landscape Studies'.

HOWARD, Peter — 'Changing taste in landscape art'. Unpublished thesis University of Exeter 1983.

HUMPHREYS, Joan — *The Life and Work of Sidney Endacott, Artist of Devon England* 1873–1918. Privately published 1977.

HUMPHREYS, Richard — *The British Landscape: Through the eye of the great artists.* Hamlyn Publishing 1990.

HUNT, Peter — *Payne's Devon: A Portrait of the County from 1790 to 1830 Through the Watercolours of William Payne.* Devon Books 1986.

HUNT, Peter (editor) — *Devon's Age of Elegance.* Devon Books 1984. Described by the diaries of the Reverend John Swete, Lady Paterson and Miss Cornish.

JAPES, David — *William Payne: A Plymouth Experience.* David Japes, Publisher 1992.

JEFFREY, Ian — *The British Landscape 1920–1950.* Thames & Hudson 1984.

KAUFFMANN, C M — *John Varley 1778–1842.* Batsford 1984.

KNOWLING, Philip — *Dartmoor: The Country Magazine* (no 9 summer 2000). Halsgrove. Contains article about Dominic Welch, sculptor.

LINDSAY, Lionel — *Conrad Martens: The Man and his Art.* Angus & Robertson, revised and enlarged edition 1968, first published 1920.

LOCKETT, Richard — *Samuel Prout 1783–1852.* Batsford 1985.

MALLALIEU, H L — *The Dictionary of British Watercolour Artists up to 1920, Vol 1 The Text.* ACC 1986, 1997 reprint.

MALLALIEU, H L — *The Dictionary of British Watercolour Artists up to 1920, Vol 2 The Plates.* ACC 1979, 1991 reprint.

MALLALIEU, Huon — *Country Life* (Vol CXCIV no 14). Has details of a record-breaking sale of a John White Abbott painting.

MESSUM, A D — *The Devonshire Scene.* David Messum Fine Paintings, Exeter 1973. Exhibition catalogue.

MILDREN, James — The *Western Morning News* (4 September 1967). Article about Charles E Brittan Jr., 'A Painter who loved the moor'.

MOORE, Andrew — *The Norwich School of Artists.* HMSO 1985, second impression 1995.

MORRIS, Susan — *Sotheby' Art at Auction 1989–90.* 'Two Girtin discoveries'. Sotheby's Publications 1990.

MUNRO, Jane — *British Landscape Watercolours 1750–1850.* Herbert Press 1994.

MURDOCH, John & others — *The Discovery of the Lake District: A Northern Arcadia and its uses.* Victoria & Albert Museum 1984. Exhibition catalogue.

OPPE, Paul — 'Francis Towne, Landscape Painter', *Walpole Society* Vol 8, 1919–20

OUSBY, Ian — *The Englishman's England; Taste, Travel and the rise of Tourism.* CUP 1990

OWEN, Felicity	*John Gendall (1789–1865) 'Exeter's Forgotten Artist'.* Exeter Museums Publication No 97 1979. Exhibition catalogue.
PEARCE, Fiona	*Cecil Arthur Hunt VPRWS RBA 1873–1965.* Chris Beetles Ltd 1996.
POLLEY, Roger & WOODMAN, John	*Spirit of Nature: Poetry of the Earth, Photographic Sketches of Devon.* Devon Books 1994. Contains a photographic survey of Bullaton Farmstead.
PYCROFT, George	*Art in Devonshire with the Biographies of Artists born in that County.* Elands, Exeter 1883. Reprints, with additions, the papers by the same author in the *Transactions* of the Devonshire Association for 1881 and 1882.
RAJNAI, Miklos	*The Norwich School of Painters.* Jarrold & Sons 1985.
RANSOM, Bill	*The Devon Historian* (no 49 October 1994). 'Devon Landscape Artists: Frederick Richard Lee'. (no 51 October 1995) 'Devon Landscape Artists: William Traies'. (no 54 April 1997) 'Devon Landscape Artists: Samuel Prout'.
REDHEAD, Brian	*The Inspiration of Landscape: Artists in National Parks.* Phaidon 1989.
RETALLICK, L	*Catalogue of Paintings on display at Torre Abbey, Torquay.* Borough of Torbay 1986 reprint.
REYNOLDS, Graham	*English Watercolours: An Introduction.* Herbert Press 1950, 1989.
REYNOLDS, Jan	*The Williams Family of Painters.* ACC 1975.
ROSENTHAL, Michael	*British Landscape Painting.* Phaidon 1982
SCRUTON, David	*New Inhabitants: Seven Artists on Dartmoor.* Exeter City Museum & Art Gallery 1993. Exhibition catalogue.
SHALGOSKY, Sarah	*The fabricated landscape: Dartmoor.* Plymouth City Museum & Art Gallery 1989. Exhibition catalogue.
SHANES, Eric	*Turner's Rivers, Harbours and Coasts.* Chatto & Windus 1981.

SHILLITO, Biddy — *Ernest Knight.* Chapel Publications 1997.

SKEAPING, John — *Drawn from Life: An Autobiography.* Collins 1977.

SKEAPING, Nicholas — *John Skeaping 1901–1980 A Retrospective.* Ackermann & Son 1991. Exhibition catalogue.

SMILES, Sam (editor) — *Going Modern and Being British: Art, Architecture and Design in Devon c.1910–1960.* Intellect Books 1998.

SMILES, Sam & PIDGLEY, Michael — *The Perfection of England: Artist Visitors to Devon c.1750–1870.* University of Plymouth 1995. Exhibition catalogue.

SMILES, Sam — Unpublished thesis 'Plymouth and Exeter as centres of art 1820–1865'. A Dissertation submitted for the PhD Degree for the University of Cambridge 1982.

SOMERS COCKS, J V — *Devon Topographical Prints 1660–1870: A Catalogue and Guide.* Devon Library Services 1977.

SWETE, John — *Travels in Georgian Devon: The Illustrated Journals of the Reverend John Swete 1789–1800.* Devon Books. Four vols, 1997, 1998, 1999, 2000. Each volume is edited and has an introduction by Todd Gray.

TORBAY CIVIC SOCIETY — *John Salter, Torquay Artist.* Eight-page leaflet. Torquay Museum, undated.

THORPE, James — *Happy Days: Recollections of an Unrepentant Victorian.* Gerald Howe Ltd 1933.

WARNER, Marina & others — *Peter Randall-Page: Sculpture and Drawings 1977–1992.* Centre for the Study of Sculpture, Henry Moore Institute 1992, reprinted 1997.

WHITE, William — *White's Devon. A Reprint of History, Gazetteer and Directory of Devonshire.* Augustus M Kelly, New York 1968.

WHYBROW, Marion — *St Ives 1883–1993: Portrait of an Art Colony.* ACC, 1994.

WILCOX, Scott & NEWALL, Christopher — *Victorian Landscape Watercolours.* Yale Center for British Art 1992. Exhibition catalogue.

WILCOX, Timothy — *Francis Towne.* Tate Gallery Publishing 1997. Exhibition catalogue.

WILSON, Roger, B — *Go Great Western: A History of GWR Publicity.* David & Charles 1970, second extended edition 1987.

WILTON, Andrew & LYLES, Anne — *The Great Age of British Watercolours 1750–1880.* Royal Academy of Arts 1993. Exhibition catalogue.

WOOD, Jeremy — *Hidden Talents: A Dictionary of Neglected Artists Working 1880–1950.* Jeremy Wood Fine Art 1994.

WOODS, Stephen — *Dartmoor Stone.* Devon Books 1988, reprinted 1999.

WOOTTON, David — *Chris Beetles Summer Show 1998.* Chris Beetles Ltd 1998.

WORMLEIGHTON, Austin — *A Painter Laureate: Lamorna Birch and his circle.* Sansom & Co/Redcliffe Press 1995.

YEATES, John — *An Endless View: The Artist and Exmoor.* Exmoor Books 1995.

Index